AF023

MASSIMILIANO AFIERO

AXIS FORCES
23

The Axis Forces number 23 – June 2023

Direction and editing: Via San Giorgio, 11 – 80021 AFRAGOLA (NA) -ITALY

Managing and Chief Editor: Massimiliano Afiero

Email: maxafiero@libero.it - **Website:** www.maxafiero.it

Contributors

Tomasz Borowski, Grégory Bouysse, Stefano Canavassi, Carlos Caballero Jurado, Rene Chavez, Gary Costello, Paolo Crippa, Carlo Cucut, Antonio Guerra, John B. Köser, Lars Larsen, Christophe Leguérandais, Eduardo M. Gil Martínez, Michael D. Miller, Danilo Morisco, Péter Mujzer, Ken Niewiarowicz, Erik Norling, Raphael Riccio, Marc Rikmenspoel, Samcevich Andrei, Hugh Page Taylor, Charles Trang, Sergio Volpe

Editorial

Here we are at the second issue of this year's magazine, with the same format as the previous one and with the same number of pages. This initiative, despite the inevitable increase in the cover price, seems to have been very well received by our readers, who seem to have liked the new editorial formula. Therefore, continue to subscribe to us, in increasing numbers, and to inform us of topics and subjects to be dealt with in future issues, in order to better respond to your needs. The greater number of pages gives us the opportunity to publish more in-depth and complete articles and above all accompanied by numerous photos and maps. As always, we will try to deal with new and little-known topics, with particular interest in the Axis volunteer formations. Let us now analyze the contents of this new issue of the magazine. We begin with a long and interesting work on the use of the Totenkopf division during the Zitadelle operation launched by the Germans to eliminate the dangerous Kursk salient. Then follows the biography of Fritz von Scholz, an officer who first served in the Wiking division and then commanded the Nordland division. We continue with the formation and use of the Italian Army on the Eastern front, a topic that we will also deal with in the upcoming issues. Speaking of Axis volunteer formations, we begin with this issue an in-depth study of the history of Swedish volunteers enlisted in the Waffen-SS. We close with the formation of the Hitlerjugend division. Always hoping to have met your interest in military history, I wish you all a good read and see you in the next issue.

Massimiliano Afiero

The Axis Forces 023 - First edition June 2023 by Luca Cristini Editor for the brand Soldiershop Cover & Art Design by soldiershop factory.   ISBN code: 978-88-93279932

Contents

Totenkopf Division and Operation Zitadelle July 1943

by Massimiliano Afiero

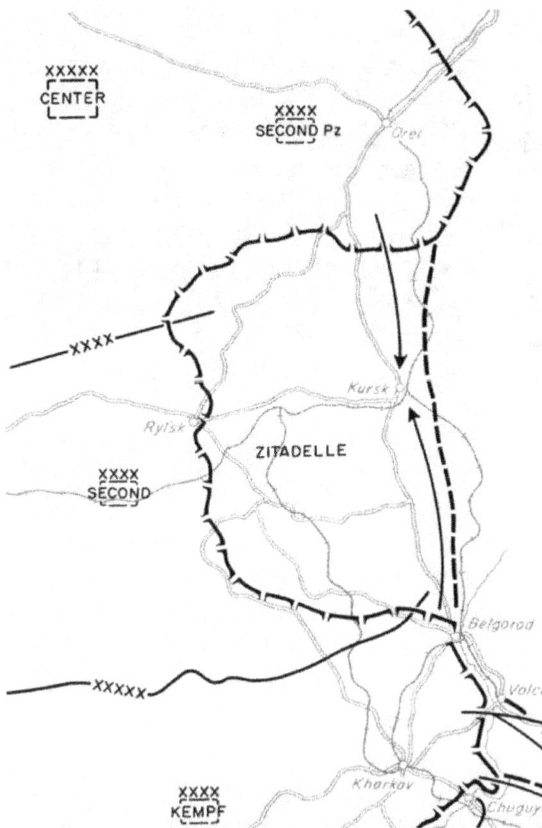

The Zitadelle pincer movement (*U.S.Army*).

A *Ferdinand* tank destroyer in field 1943.

Following the recapture of Kharkov and Bjelgorod in March 1943, the Germans had somehow managed to stave off the terrible effects of the Soviet victory at Stalingrad and above all had been able to retake much of the ground that had been lost the previous winter. The front line had been straightned but, there was only a wide salient about eighty miles deep around the city of Kursk, which was the objective of the next German offensive on the Eastern Front. As early as April, German headquarters had suggested an attack to exploit Soviet difficulties. Hitler however was opposed, undecided as to how to prosecute the war on the Eastern Front. His aggressive nature inclined him to attack, but at the same time, he wanted to be sure of success and so he postponed the start date of the offensive several times, especially to wait for production of the new *Tiger* and *Panther* tanks and of the *Ferdinand* tank destroyers. For the attack against the Kursk salient, German strategists relied on the classic pincer movement: simultaneous attacks from the north and the south to destroy the Soviet forces. The forces of von Kluge's Army Group Center were to descend from the north, and from the south, those of von Manstein's Army Group South. Considering the varying times of the thaw on the two different fronts, it was decided to postpone the offensive until the summer, a delay that was also desired by Hitler himself, who was increasingly more decided to wait for mass production of the *Tiger* and the *Panther*. On April 15, 1943, after several discussions at the German High Command, Operations Order Number 6 was issued relating to Operation *Zitadelle*. In that regard Hitler wrote: "*...This* *attack is of decisive importance. It must be immediately successful...and put the initiative in our hands. All preparations must be made with the greatest care and energy: the best units, the best weapons, the best commanders and a large quantity of ammunition will be sent to the area of the greatest effort. The victory at Kursk must serve as a beacon for the entire world".*

Adolf Hitler and his generals at the situation conference at Manstein *Heeresgruppe Süd* **in Ukraine, 1943.**

Heinz Guderian.

Most of the German generals agreed with Hitler, although Guderian, recently named Inspector General of the armored troops, was very worried about risking all of his reserves in a single offensive. Von Manstein as well, who was among the earliest supporters of the operation, began to become more cautious, advising that they should wait for the Soviet offensive and then to counterattack, repeating the action taken at Kharkov. German indecision and continuous postponement of the operation gave the Soviets all the time they needed to prepare for the new enemy move, thanks also to all of the information they were able to receive beforehand from the spy named Lucy. This enabled the Soviets, who knew the details of the plans for Operation *Zitadelle*, to reinforce their defensive preparation along the entire Kursk front: five thousand kilometers of trenches were dug along eight defensive lines, minefields were laid, anti-tank ditches were dug and artillery emplacements of all calibers were laid out. Particularly impressive was the number of anti-tank guns that were fielded, demonstrating the great fear that the Soviets held for German tanks.

Well-camouflaged Soviet anti-tank positions on Kursk front, Summer 1943.

SS-Obergruppenführer **Paul Hausser.**

Luftwaffe aerial reconnaissance photographed the smallest details of the area all around Kursk, revealing to headquarters and to the intelligence services the formidable defensive works built by the Soviets, but even that did not halt preparations for the offensive.

Employment of the SS troops

After having been pulled off the front line, the three divisions of Paul Hausser's *SS-Panzer-Korps*, the *Leibstandarte*, *Das Reich* and *Totenkopf*, were completely reorganized. Hausser's corps itself was renamed as the *II.SS-Panzer-Korps*, officially as of 1 July 1943, even though in effect it was the first large unit of the *Waffen SS*. During the months of May and June, much attention had to be given to training of thousands of new volunteers who had come from depot and training units. Rather than just volunteers, most of the personnel were conscripts and *Luftwaffe* ground personnel. New tanks, vehicles and other equipment arrived along with the new recruits. At the same time, maintenance personnel worked night and day to repair equipment that had been damaged during the previous fighting. The armored regiments of the *Waffen SS* divisions were reorganized in order to integrate the new vehicles and equipment. For example, the *Leibstandarte* and the *Das Reich* had to send their first battalions to Germany for training on the new *Panther* tanks. Unfortunately the training cycle was not completed prior to the beginning of Operation *Zitadelle*, as the *Panthers* did not reach the Eastern Front until August.

A repair point: a *Totenkopf Tiger* tank is on the left, Summer 1943 (U.S. NARA).

A *PzKpfw.III* and a *Tiger* of the *Totenkopf* Division (NA).

With respect to the *Tiger* tanks, however, each SS division still had only one "heavy" company assigned. Around the end of June, the headquarters of the *SS-Panzer-Korps* was alerted to be prepared to move to its new assembly area within a few days. On July 1, 1943 Hitler called from his headquarters in East Prussia to be updated on the state of preparations. The next day, July 2, 1943, the date for the beginning of Operation *Zitadelle*, was firmly set for July 5. The SS troops thus began to move from the Kharkov area towards Bjelgorod. The moves were mad by night in an attempt to hide the movements from the enemy as much as possible. But on the other side, the Soviets already knew everything: Marshal Georgy Zhukov was aware of the German plans and knew that the attack would probably start between July 3-6.

All of this was thanks to the British *Ultra* decoding machine, which was capable of deciperhing messages coded by the German *Enigma* machine. The Soviet commands were aware of all of the details of the operation: units involved, objectives, start date, movement of various units, all of this even before German commanders knew the details. Thanks to this useful intelligence, Zhukov was able to organize his defenses at Kursk in time. The most important Soviet success was in preventing the German panzers from breaking through the

Cleaning the barrel on *PzKpfw.IV* of the *Totenkopf* Division, Summer 1943.

A Soviet anti-tank array on the Kursk front, Summer 1943.

defensive line and maneuvering freely, owing to an impressive line of fortifications, anti-tank ditches, minefields and pak-fronts, that is, massive concentrations of anti-tank guns at specific points of the front. For about three months the Soviets employed men and machines to build a defensive line that was fully 48 kilometers in depth around the Kursk salient. Millions of mines were laid all along the defensive line and behind them thousands of anti-tank guns and cannons were emplaced. Between the various defensive lines, the Soviets deployed armored brigades that were ready to counterattack while behind the entire defensive system several armored corps were in reserve ready to deal with any possible German breakthrough.

In particular, in the sector reserved for the *SS-Panzer-Korps*, the 6th Guards Army had prepared a trap for the *Waffen SS* troops: along the attack front were two Guards rifle divisions, the 52nd and the 67th, well dug in behind a series of hills, from which they could spot the movements of the enemy in advance and direct their artillery fire.

A *Totenkopf* defensive position with an *MG-34*, Summer 1943 (U.S. NARA).

A Soviet mortar position on Kursk front, Summer 1943.

Supporting them were two anti-tank regiments and two tank regiments, well camouflaged in bunkers and revetments. A dense system of anti-tank ditches was designed to push the German tanks towards the Soviet anti-tank positions. More than a thousand machine gun nests and mortar batteries were positioned behind the minefields. In all, in the 6th Guards Army sector, there were more than four hundred 40 and 76 mm anti-tank guns, around eight hundred mortars and five hundred artillery pieces of various caliber.

The opposing forces

Considering the importance of the offensive, both sides committed substantial forces in order to achieve success, a concentration of men and machines never seen before during the course of the war. The Germans committed Model's *9.Armee* (deployed in the north) and Hoth's *4.Panzer-Armee* (supported by Kemp's armored group) in the south. Both armies were to be supported by the 6th Luftflotte (under von Greim) and by the 4th Luftflotte (under Dessloch); in all there were 900,000 men, 10,000 artillery pieces, 2,700 tanks and 1,800 aircraft. The Soviets fielded the Central Front (Marshal Rokossovsky), the Voronezh Front (Marshal Vatutin) and the Steppe Front (Marshal Konev);

Soviet infantry sheltering in a trench, Summer 1943.

A Soviet 45 mm anti-tank gun on Kursk front, 1943.

A *Totenkopf* tanker, photographed from the side hatch.

in all, 1.377,000 men, 20,000 artillery pieces, 3,300 tanks and 2,650 aircraft. The *SS-Panzer-Korps* under Paul Hausser was deployed to the south, where the *4.Panzer-Armee* and *Armee-Abteilung Kempf* were to operate, deployed respectively to the west and southeast of Bjelgorod. Facing those positions were the 6th and 7th Guards armies, protecting the two key positions of Oboyan an Korochka.

4.Panzer-Armee (*General* Hermann Hoth)

II.SS-Pz.Korps (*SS-Ogruf.* Paul Hausser)
SS-Pz.Gr.Div. Leibstandarte Adolf Hitler
SS-Panzergrenadier Division Das Reich
SS-Panzergrenadier Division Totenkopf

XLVIII.Panzer-Korps
Pz.Grenadier Division Grossdeutschland
3.Panzer Division
11.Panzer Division
167.Infanterie Division
10 Panzer Brigade
911.Sturmgeschütz Abteilung

LII.Armee-Korps
57.Infanterie Division
255.Infanterie Division
332.Infanterie Division

Armee-Abteilung Kempf, commanded by *General* Werner Kempf, consisted of:

III.Panzer-Korps (*6., 7.* and *9.Panzer Division, 168.Infanterie Division, 228.Sturmgeschütz Abteilung, 503.schwere Panzer Abteilung*)

XLII.Armee-Korps (*39., 161.* and *282.Infanterie Division, 560.Panzerjäger Abteilung*)

XI.Armee-Korps (*106.* and *320.Infanterie Division* and *393.* and *905.Sturmgeschütz Abteilung*)

Generaloberst **Hermann Hoth.**

SS-Brigdf. **Hermann Priess.**

Attack plans

Hoth's *4.Panzer-Armee* was to break through the Soviet defensive line along the Voronezh front, proceed to the northeast and capture the key position of Prokhorovka. After having eliminated enemy forces in the area, the *4.Panzer-Armee* troops were to push to the northwest, towards Kursk in order to make contact with forces of *9.Armee* under Model, coming from the north. The three divisions of Hausser's *SS-Panzer-Korps* were to attack along parallel axes in order to be able to protect each other's flanks. In order to confuse enemy intelligence services, the German command issued special orders for the armored units to use different identification markings on their vehicles. Vertical bars were adopted for the three SS divisions: two for *Das Reich*, three for the *Totenkopf* and two and a half for the *LSSAH*. On the morning of July 3, the *SS-Panzer-Korps* troops assembled in their designated positions for the beginning of the attack.

On the left, were the troops of the *Leibstandarte*, in the center those of *Das Reich* and on the right their comrades from the *Totenkopf*. Prior to midnight of July 4, engineer scout parties were sent forward to occupy vantage points for artillery observers. During those same hours, Soviet artillery had begun to shell the German positions, demonstrating that the Soviets were aware of the exact date of the beginning of the operation. Nonetheless, Operation *Zitadelle* began at dawn on July 5, 1943.

Orders for the Totenkopf

In early July, the *Totenkopf* took up positions on the front northwest of Bjelgorod. During the morning of July 1, the division was reinforced with the following artillery groups:

-*I./SS-Art.-Rgt. LSSAH* under *SS-Hstuf.* DeVries
-*II./Art.-Rgt.238*
-*He.Art.-Abt.861*
-*SS-Kp.Werfer-Abt.* under *SS-Hstuf.* des Coudres

	Stufe A	Stufe B	Stufe C
I.SS-Pz.K.	◖	¶	▲
L.SS-„A.H."	⊔⊔	⌐◗	V
SS.„D.R."	⊔⊔	⌐◉	▼
SS.„T."	|||	◼◉◼	V

The special 'markings' for the *SS-Pz.Korps* during *Zitadelle*.

Waffen SS grenadiers.

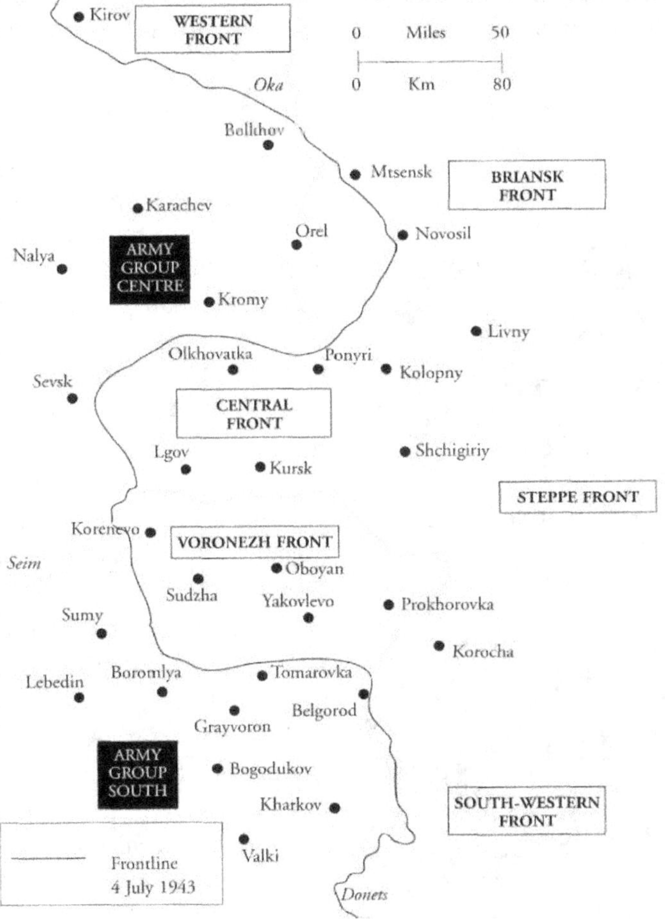

The military situation on July 4, 1943.

The orders for the division for Operation *Zitadelle*, whose kick-off was scheduled for July 5, were as follows: "...*The II.SS-Pz.Korps will attack on Day J with its center of gravity at the point of contact with the SS-Pz.Gren.Div. Das Reich and the LSSAH; after having overrun the forward enemy outposts, the forward defensive line must be penetrated in the Beresoff-Sadelnoje sector, then to push on to the second line in the Lutschki-Jakowlewo sector and with the bulk of the troops reach the area of Prochowrowka along the course of the Psel. The primary objective of the offensive is the crossing of the Psel in the Wassiljewka sector...".*

On July 3, the *Totenkopf* engineers began to clear the mines which they had laid the previous April, to clear lanes for the passing of the rest of the units at the time of the attack. On July 4, Soviet infantry was already in their positions, ready to defend against the imminent German offensive. Rain, however, hindered movement of the *Totenkopf* troops, who assumed positions on the left flank of the *II.SS-Pz.Korps*.

A *Totenkopf* officer scanning the horizon, July 1943.

SS grenadier passing by a 150 mm howitzer of the *Totenkopf*.

Tiger tanks of a German Army unit, July 1943.

The SS grenadiers reached their jump-off points during the night. *SS-Pz.Rgt.3* was at Rakowo, ready to intervene at a moment's notice; at that time it had 59 *PzKpfw III*, 47 *PzKpfw IV*, 11 *PzKpfw VI Tiger* and 8 *Bef.Pz.III* for a total of 125 operational tanks. *SS-StuG.-Abt."T"* had 28 assault guns and *SS-Pz.Jg.-Abt."T"* had 11 tank destroyers. On the eve of the offensive, the division had 164 armored vehicles and more than 21,000 men.

The offensive begins

During the night between July 4-5, the *5.Kp./"TE"* was the first unit of the division to enter action: by 2:30 its greandiers had been able to seize the Soviet outposts on Hill 218, southeast of Beresoff. Soviet artillery reacted quickly, cutting all telephone communications. An attack by Soviet infantry quickly followed. The attack was staved off, but the Germans realized that there would be no surprise effect: the Soviets were waiting for their attack. At 3:15, hundreds of artillery pieces opened fire. At 4:00, supported by *Stukas* and by a formidable shelling of the Soviet positions, the *Leibstandarte* and *Das Reich* divisions went on the attack. At 5:10, *Das Reich* troops were stalled by an anti-tank screen (*Pakfront*) in front of Beresoff, while at 6:20 the *Leibstandarte* troops had to establish defensive positions facing the western bank of the Worskla River.

A *le.IG.18* of the *SS-Pz.Korps* in position, July 1943 (U.S. NARA).

Waffen SS **grenadiers waiting for orders.**

SS-Ogruf. Paul Hausser did not wish to commit the *Totenkopf* on the right flank of the *II.SS-Pz.Korps* until Beresoff was taken. Nonetheless, *Generaloberst* Hoth ordered the division to be committed immediately; to that end, *SS-Pz.Gren.Rgt.1 "T"* was ordered to break through the enemy defensive line south fo Beresoff. The SS grenadiers crossed *"no man's land"* in single file.

At 9:15 they attacked Hill 218 with the support of assault guns and tanks. The *SS-Korps-Werfer-Abt.* had detached forward observers for artillery fire support. The *Nebelwerfer* batteries unleashed a hurricane of fire on the Soviet positions for a full hour, between 10:10 and 11:10, but despite that impressive fire support, the advance of the grenadiers continued to be slow, slowed down mainly by minefields and by enemy artillery fire. The engineers were then sent forward to clear a path for the grenadiers and the tanks; the SS engineers of *16.(Pi.)Kp./"T"* managed to open a gap in the anti-tank ditch. At 12:30 the *II./"T"* was able to get past the *Pakfront* that had blocked the advance of the *Das Reich* some hours earlier. *S-Pz.Rgt.3*, reinforced by the SPW battalion of *SS-Stubaf.*

Schneider, attacked to the northeast, suffering the loss of several armored vehicles. Near Beresoff, the *Tiger-Kompanie* commanded by *SS-Ostuf.* Schröder, after having reached Hill 216.5, continued eastwards, broke through as far as the Gonki-Belgorod Rollbahn, seized Hill 225.9 and, attacking along the Rollbahn, at 15:45 reached the Smelok Trudu Kolkhoz (collective farm). Five of the panzers suffered damaged caused by mines, among them the company commander's tank.

Waffen SS grenadiers moving up to the front to engage in battle, July 1943 (U.S. NARA).

*Nebelwerfer*s unleashing a hurricane of fire on enemy positions.

SS-StuG-Abt."T", under *SS-Hstuf*. Werner Korff, alos suffered heavy losses during the first day of the offensive; the commander of *3.Batterie, SS-Hstuf*. Linde, was killed in the fighting. At 14:35, the *I./"TE"* of *SS-Stubaf*. Knöchlein attacked north of Hill 224.3, followed at 15:00 by *III./"TE"* under *SS-Stubaf*. Kühn. The forward Soviet posts were rapidly overrun and the two SS battalions were soon engaged in clearing the woods southwest of Jerik. In the late afternoon, the bulk of the division reached the forest at Shurawlinyj, from the Gremutschi Valley.

During the night between July 5-6, fighting continued and casualties continued to mount. At 3:45, *SS-Kampfgruppe Häussler*, consisting of the *II./"T"* and the *Tiger-Kompanie*, attacked Hill 225.9. The *Tigers* were taken under fire by an anti-tank position situated west of Ternowka. *SS-Stubaf*. Kunstmann, commander of *SS-Pz.Rgt.3*, ordered his engineer company to eliminate the threat. *SS-Ostuf*. Georg Kinzler, charged with the mission, was given as support a tank platoon with four *PzKpfw III* : "...*Riding on the panzers, we drove almost two kilometers to the east along the road* [Bjelgorod-Kursk]. *Now we had to determine where the enemy strongpoint was.*

Totenkopf tanks and half-tracks during an attack northwards, July 1943.

A *PzKpfw.III* followed by an *SdKfz.250* on the march.

Assaulting with an *MG-42*.

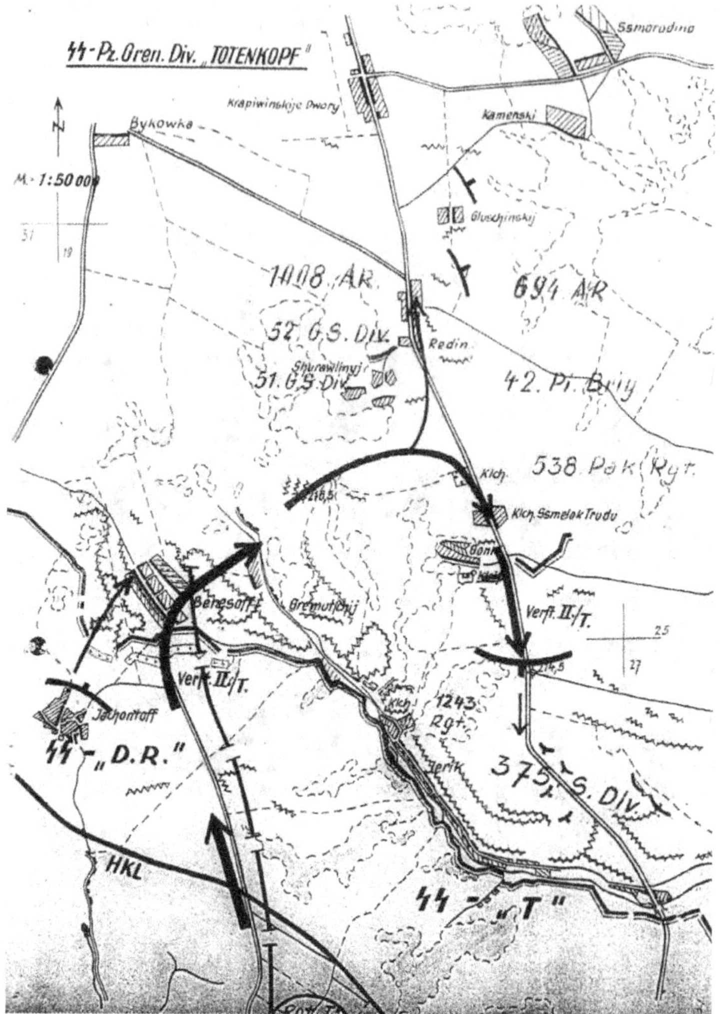

Totenkopf movements on July 5, 1943.

Assault guns of *SS-StuG-Abt. 'T'* on the move (U.S. NARA).

This was protected by an infantry position. We got off the panzers and began to advance in two groups (the panzers stayed behind). The group on the left was led by SS-Ustuf. Arthur Dähnert, the group on the right by myself. Up until then, we did not see the Soviets.

The ground, with ripe grain and high grass, hid us well. Without being seen, we got to within about a hundred meters of the enemy position. As we had agreed with the panzer crews, I fired a flare into the air. Their guns opened fire immediately. For us it was the signal to attack! We broke into the enemy positions under cover of fire from the tanks. The Soviets were taken by surprise. Some of the crews raised their hands and surrendered, others attempted to flee. We captured the position after close-quarter fighting. One of the three anti-tank guns fell intact into our hands. Some engineers then pointed the gun towards Terenowka. A captured Soviet lieutenant explained to us how it worked. But enemy artillery had already begn to shell the hill. We had completed our mission and there was no longer any reason to hang around. After having left a forward group on the spot, we returned to out panzers. We hoisted two of our comrades who had fallen in the fighting onto our shoulders".

In the meantime, the division's armored group, consisting of *II./SS-Pz.Rgt.3* and *I.(gep.)/"T"*, attacked to the northeast.

A German panzer column on the move on the Kursk front, July 1943.

A column of Tiger tanks on the move, July 1943.

A column of *Totenkopf Stug.III* on the move, July 1943.

SS-Uscha. Stettner, a *5.Kp.* tank commander, noted in his diary : "*After having crossed the anti-tank ditch, we assumed a combat formation and advanced. To our left was the 6.Kompanie led by SS-Ostuf. Westphal. We crossed a balka and passed onto a small hill. In front of us was flat gound covered with grass, then on the other side, the Lip.Donetz Valley. We spotted a village; we checked our maps, it must be Nepchajewo. We could see only the roofs of the isbas. Behind the village was a tree-covered slope. Some rounds came from there; anti-tank guns! We responded to the fire. The Soviet guns replied. Large-caliber rounds ended up among the panzers. An attack against that artillery and those anti-tank guns would have been suicide. The order was given to fire smoke rounds. We withdrew to regroup under the cover of a hill. My tank's engine had been hit and had to be repaired. I informed my platoon leader, SS-Ostuf. Burgschultze, of the situation. The Soviet artillery fire slacked off. Only an occasional round fell here and there. I withdrew to the closest village. There, we were able to repair the tank. The SPW battalion crossed our path, making a lot of noise with its tracks*".

Totenkopf tanks halted on the steppe, prior to a new attack, July 1943.

PzKpfw.IV of the *Totenkopf* climbing out of an anti-tank ditch.

The unit which Stettner refers to was the motorized group that the division had sent towards Lutschki to make contact with *Das Reich*. At that time, the *Totenkopf* troops were split into three groups which were fighting, one to the west of Schopino, another to the west of Ternowka and the last to the west of Nepchajewo. *SS-Oberführer* Priess had only one other unit still available, the reconnaissance group, whose company commanders had gathered at Gluschinskyj, at *SS-Stubaf.* Kron's command post. An enemy shell landed right on top of them; Otto Kron was gravely wounded and there were also numerous deaths.

That afternoon, troops of the *Das Reich* managed to break through the enemy's second defensive line. The Soviets reacted immediately, getting their 2nd Tank Corps to cross the Lipowyj Donetz, thus threatening the right flank of *II./SS-Pz.Korps*, whose leading units had advanced about twenty kilometers.

A column of *PzKpfw.III* tanks of the *Totenkopf* in a Ukrainian village, July 1943.

A *Totenkopf* assault gun (U.S. NARA).

Around 13:00, the two grenadier regiments of the *Totenkopf* made contact, forming a small pocket around Jerik, where Soviet troops were resisting desperately. It took the SS troops several hours to capture the place, despite fire support by *SS-Werfergruppe Nickmann*. The Soviets counterattacked without letup. All of them were driven off by fire from *5.Bttr./SS-Werfer-Abt.* led by *SS-Ostuf.* Schänzlin, equipped with four 80 mm *Vielfachwerfer*. At 16:15, *Werfergruppe Wolters* shifted its position to support the *5.Batterie*. Around 17:00, the leading elements of the 2nd Tank Corps began to attack the right flank of the *II./SS-Pz.Korps*: an armored formation consisting of about thirty tanks was spotted in the Soschenkoff sector. The *Totenkopf* was then ordered by the corps to "*...form a Sperrverband , to be employed to the east, to eliminate the enemy bridgehead and to prevent any advance by Soviet troops*". The *5.Kp./SS-Pz.Rgt.3* quickly intercepted the enemy spearhead, engaging it.

At 19:10, the *Totenkopf* reported that it had destroyed fifteen tanks, among which were twelve *Churchills*, without suffering any losses.

in World War Two 1939-1945

Waffen-SS Nebelwerfer **batteries under enemy fire, July 1943 (U.S. NARA).**

***Totenkopf* grenadiers with an *MG-42*.**

That same day, however, *SS-Stubaf.* Rudolf Schnieder, commander of *I./SS-Pz.Gr.Rgt.1"T"*, fell in battle. At dawn on 7 July, the *Totenkopf* attacked the Soviet tank concentration deployed on the western bank of the Lipowyj Donetz with *II./SS-Pz.Rgt.3* and *I.(gep.)"T"*. The SS troops were, however, driven back by Soviet artillery fire. *SS-Werfergruppe Nickmann* then arrived to support the *SS-Pz.Gren.Rgt."T"* attack. Around 10:30, Otto Baum's men reached the hills west of Lipowyj Donetz. Eleven Soviet tanks were destroyed during that fighting. At 16:30, considering that the threat to its left flank had been driven off, the headquarters of *II.SS-Pz.Korps* ordered that *le.Art.-Abt.III.818* be detached from the divison and be subordinated to the *Das Reich*. At 19:00, the *Totenkopf* reported that it had been subjected to 73 air attacks during the day.

Command of *StuG-Abt. "T"* was assigned to *SS-Hstuf.* Ernst Dehmel after Walter Korff was wounded. At 23:50, *II./SS-Pz.Korps* issued orders for the following day: the *Totenkopf* was to be relieved by the *167.Inf.Div.* for commitment on the corps left, as it seemed impossible for the *Das Reich* and *Leibstandarte* to break through without its help.

SS-Ogruf. Paul Hausser at the Totenkopf command post to discuss the situation with *SS-Oberführer* Hermann Priess and *SS-Ostubaf*. Otto Baum (seen from behind), July 1943.

A column of *PzKpfw.III* tanks advancing to the front line.

The *Totenkopf* then began to assemble part of its forces during the night between July 7-8. The armored regiment assembled at Gonki and the *I.(gep.)"T"*, led by *SS-Hstuf*. Rosenow, was relieved by *Pi.-Btl.627*. During the morning of July 8, the *Das Reich* and the *Leibstandarte* went on the attack, aiming north and northeast. The Soviets reacted by throwing powerful armored forces against the right flank of the *II.SS-Pz.Korps*, thus threatening to cut off the two SS divisions from their rear areas. At 12:45, the *Totenkopf* reported: *"Enemy attack with thirty to forty tanks and some infantry from Wisloje and Ternowka, in a westerly direction"*. The division quickly launched a counterattack with *SS-Pz.Rgt.3*, the *StuG-Abt."T"* and the *II./"TE"*. *SS-Ostuf*. Kinzler participated in the attack: *"Because of the confused situation, our commander, SS-Stubaf. Kunstmann, led the way with his Befehlspanzer, accompanied by two radio vehicles. Protection was provided by elements of my company and by men of the regimental headquarters.*

A *Tiger* returns to the rear after having suffered combat damage, while infantrymen of *Totenkopf* and *Gren.Rgt.315* head to the front. In the background are the effects of enemy artillery fire.

A *PzKpfw.III Ausf. L of Totenkopf SS-Pz.Rgt.3.*

This security force, led by me, consisted of 3 NCOs and 17 soldiers. Hanging onto the panzers, we we threw ourselves into an attack to the east, without worrying about enemy tanks that were closing in. We suddenly became the targets of enemy infantry fire coming from the hills located about 150-180 meters to our left... According to information on our maps, there were supposed to be elements of the Eicke Regiment there, but that did not seem possible. Under the protection of fire from our panzers, our security group attacked an entrenched enemy position, surrounded it and captured eight prisoners. Almost twice that number of Soviet soldiers was killed during the fighting. We continued our advance. I left an NCO and five soldiers with a sidecar on the hill to the left to provide protection for our movements. On the right, the ground was fairly open, easily providing good visibility. Around three hundred meters to our right, a large 'breast' obscured our view. According to the map, behind it should have been the Balka, an inlet of the neck of the Wisloje. The commander ordered "Halt! Absitzen!" (Halt, get off the vehicles!"). He wanted to go forward by himself to take a look at the ground.

Tiger **tanks advancing. On the right, a grenadier with an** *MG-34,* **July 1943.**

SS-Stubaf. **Kunstmann on the Kursk front.**

The two accompanying tanks stopped to the right and left behind us. Our protection group spread out across the ground. The commander's tank moved ahead slowly. After about forty meters, it stopped suddenly. At the same time, there was a deafening explosion. Shell fragments flew around the turret. The driver got out of the tank screaming: "The commander is dead, the tank is on fire". *I rushed to the driver who was waving at us. The panzer was no longer burning. We drew slowly closer. I hid on the left, to determine where the round had come from...I then spotted the enemy position, about three hundred meters away on a ridge that dominated the gorge of Wisloje, with cannons and anti-tank rifles. In the meantime, the driver had come to his senses and had climbed back into his tank to salvage it. We fired to provide cover for him. On the Soviet side, all was quiet. The panzer turned back and made its way to the two radio vehicles. I then climbed aboard the panzer and looked inside the turret. At least two rounds had penetrated and had killed the commander. We reported his death to the division by radio".*

Grenadiers and Tiger tanks, waiting to resume the attack on Kursk front, July 1943.

A *Waffen SS* grenadier on Kursk front.

Command of *SS-Pz.Rgt.3* passed to *SS-Stubaf*. Bochmann, who in turn was replaced as commander of *II.Abteilung* by *SS-Hstuf*. Fritz Biermeier. Around noon, the Tigers were faced against a massive attack by about thirty enemy tanks, near the gorge of Wisloje and Ternowka. After having knocked out two *T-34* tanks, the *Chefpanzer* was moving across a field of grain when suddenly groups of Soviet infantry surrounded the tank. *SS-Ostuf*. Schröder ordered the gunner, Ludwig Lachmann, to open fire with the turret MG, not taking into account that in the command tank another radio had been installed in place of the MG. When he realized his mistake, he ordered the radio operator to open fire. But, after a few bursts, his gun jammed. Schröder then yelled at his gunner to give him his machine pistol; he opened the turret hatch and began to fire on the enemy sodiers. After having emptied several magazines, he fell into the tank covered with blood. He had been hit in the head by an anti-tank rifle round. Thanks to the machine gun fire by the radio operator, who had resumed firing, and a few hand grenades, the enemy infantry withdrew. *SS-Ustuf*. Walter Köhler then assumed command of the Tiger company. At 14:00, the division issued the following report: *"The armored regiment, minus one battalion, is fighting against enemy tanks 1.2 km east of Hill 209.5 and against a battalion that is withdrawing towards Ternowka. The assault gun group is advancing from Hill 209.5 to the north, towards the gorge to the west of Wisloje where an enemy battalion is located. Several enemy tanks spotted 2 km northeast of Gonki"*. To the west of Wisloje the Soviet troops, despite being supported by about thirty tanks, were pushed back across the Lipowyj Donetz, suffering heavy losses.

StuG.III of the Totenkopf advancing with infantry loaded on board, on the march (U.S. NARA).

A *Totenkopf* grenadier, July 1943 (NA).

The *Totenkopf* was not the only unit to experience counterattacks by Soviet tanks: on the afternoon of July 8, the entire *II.SS.Pz.Korps* had to assume a defensive stance. The Soviet objective of blocking the advance of *II.SS.Pz.Korps* at all costs was thus achieved. The German commands had to call upon all of their reserves to hold off the enemy counterattacks. And thus, *II./SS-Pz.Rgt.3* and *SS-Pz.Aufkl.-Abt."T"* had to be sent to support the troops of *Das Reich*, heavily engaged in the area south of Lutschki.

That same afternoon, the leading units of the *167.Infanterie-Division* began to arrive to relieve the *Totenkopf*, allowing them to give new impetus to the *II.SS.Pz.Korps* offensive. The division was to eastablish a bridgehead on the Psel River, in the Krasnyj Oktjabr-Koslowka sector. Artillery support was to be provided by *III./Werfer-Rgt.55*.

The bridgehead on the Psel

During the night between July 8-9, the *Totenkopf* assumed positions in the Teterewino-Lutschki area. The Soviets, however, did not stay idle: at 2:15 they attacked with fifteen tanks southwest of Wisloje. *SS-StuG-Abt."T"* and the *II./"TE"* staved off the attack.

SS-Oberführer **Priess and** *SS-Ostubaf.* **Otto Baum discussing the latest orders (U.S. NARA).**

Totenkopf **grenadiers ready to attack, July 1943 (U.S. NARA).**

At 7:55 the Soviets attacked the *Totenkopf* positions northeast of Teterewino with about thirty tanks, but they were repulsed by the grenadiers of the *III./"TE"*. At 10:00, *Kampfgruppe Baum*, consisting of *SS-Pz.Gren.Rgt.1 "T"* and *II./SS-Pz.Rgt.3*, finally attacked, reaching Wesselyj at 11:15. The *II./SS-Pz.Rgt.3* then proceded towards the hills located to the east of Kotschetowka. A quarter of an hour later, it found itself dealing with a Soviet armored unit. At 12:50, tanks of the *Totenkopf* found themselves up against about sixty Soviet tanks east of Gresnoje. At 15:30 the *I.* and *II./"TE"* attacked towards Krasnyj Oktjabr in order to establish a bridgehead on the Psel. At 18:45, the *I./"TE"* captured Koslowka, but enemy resistance intensified as soon as the SS units neared the river. Soviet artillery shelled all of the access routes incessantly. It was then decided to wait until dark to attempt to cross the Psel. At that time the division had 48 *PzKpfw III*, 28 *PzKpfw IV*, 1 *PzKpfw VI Tiger*, 5 *Bef.Pz.*, 21 *StuG III* and 11 *Marder II*, for a total of 114 armored vehicles, practically fifty tanks less than were available at the beginning of the campaign.

Totenkopf **tanks and infantry south of Psel, July 1943 (U.S. NARA).**

A *Waffen SS* grenadier, July 1943 (NA).

For the *Totenkopf*, the orders for that day called for the establishment of a bridgehead on the Psel and then to seize Beregowoje and the hills northwest of that location. Crossing of the river was to be effected with equipment of the *Pi.-Rgt.-Stab z.b.V. 680* and with the support of the *SS-Korps-Werfer-Abteilung*.

During the night between July 9-10, the engineers and grenadiers prepared for the next day's attack. Soviet aircraft bombed their forward posts. In addition, violent rainstorms transformed the roads into bogs, making the work of the engineers and the arrival of supplies even more difficult. At 4:00, the reconnaissance group arrived to cover the left flank of *II.SS-Pz.Korps* towards Kotschetowka. At 10:00, the *Eicke* Regiment, on the right, and the *Totenkopf* Regiment, on the left, attacked. The SS grenadiers could see the villages of Bogorodizkoje and Kljutschi, situated on the northern bank of the Psel. On the other side were hills covered with forests and deep gullies. On those hills, the muzzle flashes of Soviet artillery were perfectly visible. The German advance was stalled almost immediately; SS troop losses were very high. In the afternoon, the weather improved around 15:00 and the *Totenkopf* was able to resume its attack.

SS grenadiers advancing in the hills in the Psel area, July 1943 (U.S. NARA).

SS grenadiers avancing while panzers climb the hill, July 1943.

This time it was up to the *Eicke* Regiment to establish a bridgehead on the Psel. Despite dogged Soviet resistance, the *I./"TE"* was able to cross the river north of Prochorowka around 15:15. *SS-Stubaf.* Knöchlein's grenadiers seized the first Soviet positions following furious close-quarter fighting. Every foxhole and every trench was fought over. The engineers enabled reinforcements to cross the river on rubber rafts; for the time being, the heavy weapons remained on the southern bank. After several hours of hard fighting, the bridge and the village of Prochorowka were in the hands of the SS troops. At 17:00, Becker's men advance about eight hundred meters north of the Psel, expanding the bridgehead. Meanwhile, the *Totenkopf* Regiment, supported by several tanks and assault guns, was busy seizing Kljutschi. The appearance of *Stukas* put the Soviets on the run and the town was seized around 18:00. On the left flank, the *III./"T"* captured Krasnyj Oktjabr.

Totenkopf Tigers, StuG.III and *SPW* **advancing on the steppe, July 1943 (U.S. NARA).**

The *1.Kp./SS-Pi.-Btl. "T"* was then ordered to repair the bridge over the Psel that was on the northwest edge of the village. Thus, during the day, the *Totenkopf* finally managed to cross the Psel, the last natural obstacle on the road to Kursk. It was a great victory, because the Soviets had particularly reinforced their defenses in this critical sector. During the night between July 10-11, the Soviets made numerous attacks against the German bridgehead with the support of massive artillery fire. Particularly hard hit were the positions north of Koslowska, on Hill 226.6, northwest of Kljutschi and northwest of Kotschetowka. At the same time, Soviet artillery fire hindered reinforcement of the bridgehead, halting the work of the engineers. At 6:17, the *Totenkopf* reported that *"In the right-hand sector of the bridgehead, Soviet infantry was within hand grenade range of our positions. Other enemy units, of regimental strength, arrived from Wesselyj"*. At 7:50, the *Totenkopf* sent the following radio message to the headquarters of II.SS-Pz.Korps: *"Attack at 8:00 from the bridgehead still not possible, because construction of the bridge has not yet begun"*. At 8:30, the *SS-Korps-Werfer-Abteilung* was subordinated to the *III./SS-Art.-Rgt."T"* to support the attack by Becker's men.
Construction of the bridge did not begin until 8:30, with the help of tanks used as tractors to tow the equipment. At 12:30, the *Totenkopf* units that were in the bridgehead attacked in order to expand it.

From the left: *SS-Stubaf*. Haussler, Bochmann and Ullrich, in the brigdehead on the Psel.

Panzers and *StuG.IIIs* attacking towards Kljutschi.

At 14:00, the bridge at Koslowka was ready. The *I./SS-Pz.Rgt.3* then had to cross to the northern bank of the Psel, but at the same time a Soviet armored attack against Wassiljewka forced it to change its plans. That attack was driven off around 14:40. At 14:45, the panzers were ordered to cross over to the opposite bank. Plans had been made to resupply the units engaged north of the Psel, but it continued to rain and only tracked vehicles were able to move through the mud. The attack was therefore postponed until the following day. In the evening, the leading elements of *SS-Pz.Rgt.3* arrived at the bridgehead.

The battle for Prochorowka

On July 12, in an attempt to stop the *II.SS-Pz.Korps* offensive, the Soviets called upon the 5th Guards Tank Army commanded by General Pavel Rotmistrov, until then held in reserve. That army consisted of two tank corps and a mechanized corps, with more than seven hundred tanks and assault guns: during the night, Soviet artillery and aircraft had already hit the *Totenkopf* bridgehead. The positions of *SS-Art.-Rgt."T"* and of the *SS-Korps-Werfer-Abt.*

were likewise hit. Meanwhile, the intelligence services were reporting that the Soviets were committing fresh forces against the left flank of the *Totenkopf* from the Wesselyj-Ilinski sector. At 3:15, a Soviet battalion attacked the *I./"T"* positions west of Kljutschi. At 5:00, the *Leibstandarte* reported that the forward elements of its armored regiment had run up against powerful enemy tank formations.

A *PzKpfw.III Ausf.M* of the *Totenkopf* in the valley of the Psel, July 1943 (U.S. NARA).

A *Waffen SS* grenadier, July 1943.

The decisive battle was about to begin south of Prochorowka. At dawn, the *Totenkopf* informed the *4.Panzer-Armee* headquarters that its armored regiment still fielded 54 *PzKpfw III*, 30 *PzKpfw IV*, 10 *PzKpfw.VI Tiger* and 7 *Befehls-Pz.* At 6:30, the *I./SS-Pz.Rgt.3* counterattacked west of Kljutschi. Its intervention allowed the *I./"T"* to hold its positions. But an hour later, the attacks continued: at 7:30, there was fighting west of Kljutschi, and at 7:40 a Soviet battalion advanced from Ilinskij towards the Psel; at 7:45, two Soviet infantry regiments supported by forty tanks faced off against the *Eicke* Regiment in the Wassiljewka area. At the same time, on the right flank of *II.SS-Pz.Korps*, the *Das Reich* was facing strong Soviet forces. The offensive towards Prochorowka was delayed. At 9:00, the whole of *SS-Pz.Rgt.3* crossed over to the north bank of the Psel. At 9:30, *II./SS-Pz.Rgt.3* made an attack agakinst Hill 226.6.

in World War Two 1939-1945

A group of *PzKpfw.IV* of the *Totenkopf* in the Psel area, July 1943.

A *Totenkopf* artillery observer, July 1943.

Following is the testimony of *SS-Uscha*. Stettner : *"As soon as we began to march, a multitude of T-34 tanks headed straight at us at great speed. The enemy tanks got to within a hundred meters, and some within fifty meters, from us. My gunner yelled "Ready!". I then shouted "Fire!".*

Our round made a direct hit on a tank that was nearing us. There was a blinding flash and a monstrous explosion. The shock wave made our panzer jump. Steel shards whistled above us. The T-34 had literally exploded…pieces of the drive train, weighing more than a hundred kilos, were thrown a great distance through the air. We were able to stop this attack that had caught us by surprise. In front of them the engineers had suffered heavy losses. They climbed aboard the tanks with satchel charges to destroy them. There was no cover near the exploding tanks. Some engineers were killed by the steel fragments that flew about in all directions. Our battalion formed up for a counterattack. It was followed shortly thereafter by the II.Abteilung. During the advance, our company was ordered to go to the rescue of 1.Kompanie, on the right flank. The company was stalled below a hill on which there was a Soviet anti-tank position. A few of our tanks had already been knocked out. We saved our comrades and offered covering fire to the surviving crews, among which was that of my friend, Heinrich Prenzel, who were in the immobilized panzers, until our infantry troops arrived. We returned to our battalion soon after".

A *PzKpfw.III Ausf.J* passing by an *SdKfz.251* towing a *Pak 38*, July 1943.

An SS machine gunner with an *MG-42*, amidst the ruins of Soviet vehicles, July 1943.

The fighting cost the SS troops dearly. The situation was so serious that the lightly wounded were not transferred to the rear, but stayed to fight in the front line. The crews that had lost their tanks reported immediately to their company commanders, hoping to be assigned quickly to another vehicle. The Soviets continued to throw their forces into the battle, with the aim of wiping out the *Totenkopf* units that were south of the Psel in order to isolate and surround the forces that had crossed over to the northern bank of the river.

A formation of attacking self-propelled guns, July 1943.

A German tank formation attacking, July 1943.

The *II.* and *III./"TE"* were engaged in bitter defensive fighting. At 11:00, the division reported that the enemy attack that had been mounted from Wassiljewka with two regiments and about fifty tanks had been pushed back. But soon after, the Soviets returned to attack again in the sector south of Wesselyj and Ilinskij. Aerial reconnaissance spotted fresh Soviet units coming from the Obojan area. At 11:15, the *II.SS-Pz.Korps* ordered the *Totenkopf* to try to cross the Psel at Michailowka and to envelop the enemy forces south of the river, taking them from the rear. Considering the superiority of the enemy forces and the weather conditions, the action seemed very optimistic. The men had to find their own ammunition and hand grenades and bring them up to the front. In the meantime, the division's armored group continued its attack to the northeast.

The *5.Kp./SS-Pz.Rgt.3*, lacking infantry support, found itself right in the middle of a Soviet position; one of its tanks was hit and caught fire. While abandoning the tank, the crew was taken under enemy automatic weapons fire. The other panzers were attacked by Soviet infantry with Molotov cocktails. However, the SS troops reacted quickly; one of the tanks advanced slowly towards the Soviet machine gun nests. The gunner passed some hand grenades to the tank commander who popped out of the turret and threw them at the enemy positions. The machine guns were silenced one after another. The survivors surrendered and were directed to the rear area.

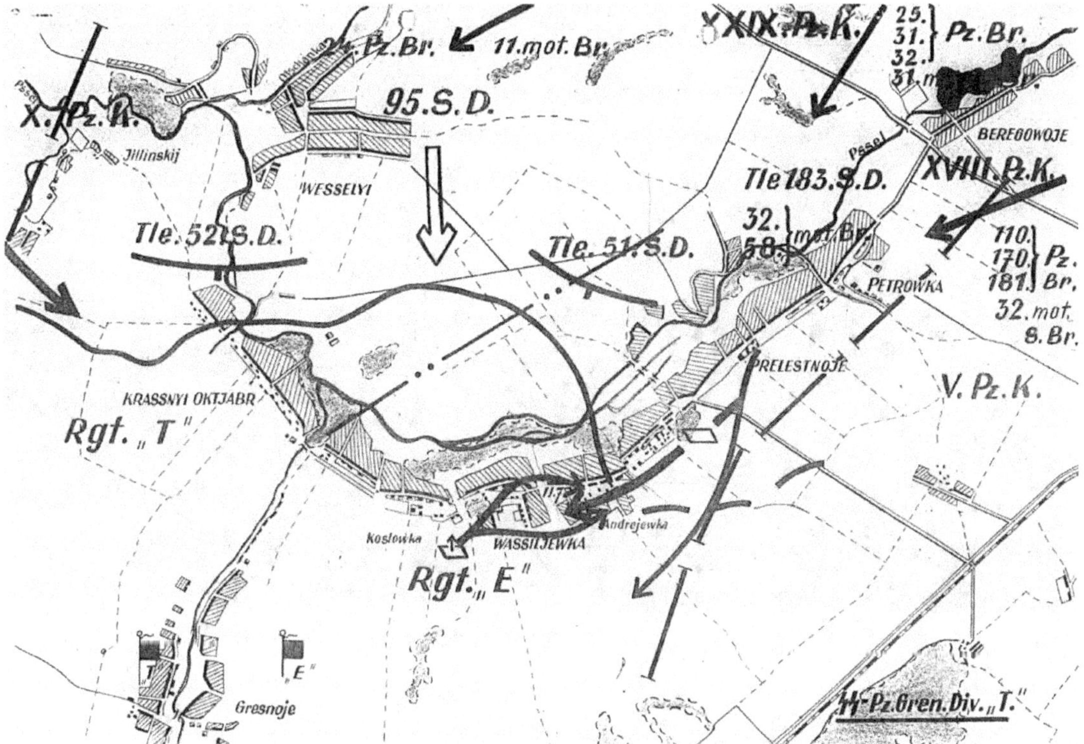

The *Totenkopf* bridgehead on the Psel River, July 1943.

A view of the battlefield from the turret of a *Panzer*.

Around 15:00, the armored group continued its attack to the northwest of Poleshajew. The *Totenkopf* suffered heavy losses: the grenadier companies were down to about a hundred effectives. Divison headquarters then decided to reinforce with recruits from the depot battalion that was located south of Snamenka. The unit was practically disbanded. At 16:45, on the division's right flank, the I./"TE" captured Andrejewka. That afternoon the *Totenkopf* troops limited their activity to reinforcing the positions they had reached.

Towards evening, the armored group continued its advance, along the way encountering a new perfectly camouflaged enemy position. Soviet artillery did not hesitate to shell its own infantry units as long as it stopped the advance of the panzers! The *Totenkopf* armored troops were forced to withdraw and to shift to a new attack position on slightly hilly ground. Anti-tank guns opened fire from a hill on the other side. Thus began a terrible firefight at a range of five hundred meters. The Soviet unit was wiped out within a few minutes: the shredded bodies of the crews and the remnants of the Soviet guns littered the ground.

Waffen SS **grenadier on a defensive position with an** *MG-42,* **July 1943.**

A *PzKpfw.III* **command tank on the Psel front, July 1943.**

Around 20:00, other Soviet tanks appeared and fresh fighting flared up on the hills northwest of Polashejew; the Soviet 31st Tank Corps was destroyed and the *Totenkopf* armored group continued its northeasterly advance. At 22:45 it reached the Beregowoje-Kartaschewka road and anchored its defense there. *SS-Ustuf.* Köhler was killed in the latest round of fighting, so that command of the *Totenkopf Tiger* company passed to *SS-Ustuf.* Karl Schüffler. General Hoth, commander of *4.Panzer-Armee*, congratulated the division for this success, which would allow the offensive to continue on towards Kursk.

Von Manstein also congratulated the units of *II.SS-Pz.Korps* for having wiped out the 5th Guards Tank Army in front of Prochorowka, even though that victory could not be exploited because of the lack of success of *III.Pz.Korps* on the right flank of Hausser's corps. The *Das Reich* was thus unable to go to the aid of the *Leibstandarte* in order to seize Prochorowka and completely wipe out the 5th Guards Tank Army, which would have put the Soviet units which were north of the Psel, facing the Totenkopf, in serious difficulty.

Waffen SS grenadiers armed with *MG-42*, following a *Marder III*, July 1943.

A *StuG.III* of the *Totenkopf* on the Ukrainian front, July 1943.

The offensive comes to a halt

That day was decisive for the fate of the offensive, because in the Orel sector the Bryansk Front had gone on the attack against 2.*Panzer-Armee*, thus threatening the rear areas of Model's 9.*Armee*. Consequently, Model was forced to go on the defensive, after having to send reinforcements to 2.*Panzer-Armee*. Operation *Zitadelle*, whose objective had been to surround Soviet forces in the Kursk salient, could now be considered to be over, with the arrest of the offensive in the northern sector. To the south, there was still the prospect that the Germans could destroy the Soviet armies that faced the 4.*Panzer-Armee* and *Armee-Abteilung Kempf*. The night between July 12-13 passed relatively quietly. In the morning, the Soviets attacked the positons of the *Eicke* Regiment, supported by only eight tanks, which reflected the heavy losses that had been incurred during the previous days. Around 10:00, many local penetrations were reported. The *I./"T"* was thrown into a counterattack.

SS-Hstuf. **Ernst Dehmel with the** *Ritterkreuz.*

A *Totenkopf Tiger* **with its crew taking a break.**

The Soviet units were forced back, but at the cost of heavy casualties. At the same time, the Soviets attempted to cut off contact between the *Totenkopf* and the *11.Panzer-Division,* attacking the positions held by *SS-Pz.Aufkl.-Abt. "T"* at Kotschetowka. The SS scouts defended themselves doggedly, but at 10:45 another Soviet regiment supported by tanks joined the attack, moving from the Wesselyj area. The *I./"T"* grenadiers tried to stem its advance, but in the end had to fall back because of the strong enemy pressure, losing eight *SPW* during the move. The self-propelled guns of *SS-StuG-Abt. "T"* were finally able to block the Soviet troops: the *StuG III* assault guns led by *SS-Hstuf.* Ernst Dehmel were engaged in a series of counterattacks against Soviet armored formations, managing to destroy fully forty-seven enemy tanks during two days of combat. During the fierce encounters, *SS-Hstuf.* Dehmel was himself seriously wounded for the sixth time since the beginning of the war. Having lost sight of one eye, deaf in one ear, and one arm amputated at the shoulder, Dehmel ended up as an instructor at the assault gun school in Janowitz in the Protectorate of Bohemia and Moravia. On August 15, 1943, Dehmel was awarded the Knight's Cross upon the recommendation of *SS-Brigdf.* Hermann Priess.

Meanwhile, *II.SS-Pz.Korps* had decided to shift its efforts to its right flank, committing *Das Reich* to an attack, because concentrating to the north of the Psel made no sense and Prochorowka was outside the *Leibstandarte's* range. The Psel sector thus became secondary. Around noon, the Soviets sought to eliminate the bridgehead and threw fresh troops into the battle without letup.

A 75mm *Pak 40* anti-tank gun of the *Totenkopf* on Kursk front, July 1943.

A wounded SS grenadier.

All of their attacks were repulsed by the SS troops. The *2.Kp./SS-Pz.Jg.-Abt."T"* led by *SS-Ustuf.* Hans Jendges particularly distinguished itself by destroying thirty-eight enemy tanks in less than twenty minutes. For that action and for having already distinguished himself previously in combat, *SS-Ustuf.* Jendges was awarded the German Cross in Gold. But losses were also high for the Germans. At 12:45, the Soviets threw their troops into another attack, without regard for their losses. The *III./"TE"*, which was defending Hill 226.6, found itself at the center of the fighting. Attacked by tanks, its grenadiers had only magnetic mines to defend themselves. *SS-Pz.Rgt.3* had to intervene.

The Soviet attack was driven off, but the armored regiment incurred losses: the ten Tigers that were engaged were all put out of action, as were two command tanks, twenty-one *PzKpfw III* and thirteen *PzKpfw IV*. Personnel losses were equally high. But, at 18:45, the division reported to *II.SS-Pz.Korps*: *"Breach closed. Previous front line re-established. Our Luftwaffe has not yet shown up"*. The attacks by the 31st Tank Corps and the 33rd Guards Rifle Corps ran up against fierce defense by the SS troops: 61 armored vehicles were destroyed by the *Totenkopf* during the course of the day, out of a total of 249 claimed by *II.SS-Pz.Korps*. Following the terrible battle, the division was left with 32 *PzKpfw III*, 17 *PzKpfw IV* and 5 *Bef.Pz.* still operational. In all, *II.SS-Pz.Korps* still had 187 panzers.

An *MG-34* used as an antiaircraft weapons on the Psel front, July 1943.

***PzKpfw.III* of *II.SS-Pz.Korps* moving with infantry on board, July 1943.**

On the left, *XLVIII.Pz.Korps* counted 173 operational tanks, and on the right *III.Pz.Korps* still had 83 tanks running. To that total, more than a hundred assault guns and tank destroyers must be added. Von Manstein thus still had over 500 tanks and could also benefit from reinforcement by *XXIV.Pz.Korps* which had been held in reserve in the Izjum area. He could thus still destroy the remnants of the 1st Tank Army and the 6th Guards Army, but Hitler decided to end Operation *Zitadelle* and send a strong political message, thinking to send the *II.SS-Pz.Korps* to Italy, where the military (and political) situation had been significantly

A *Totenkopf* **machine gun team with an** *MG-34* **and face masks, July 1943.**

SS-Ostubaf. **Otto Baum with an Army officer.**

exacerbated following the Allied landings in Sicily.On July 14, the Soviets bombarded the bridgehead on the Psel for the entire morning. Calm returned after noon, after two attacks had been fended off by the SS troops.

On July 15, Soviet artillery resumed shelling the division's positions on the bridgehead. Around 11:00, the Soviets attacked Hill 266.6 with an infantry company and only three tanks. They were easily driven off. In the evening there were other encounters on the division's left flank. At 22:00, the *Totenkopf* received the following order from *II.SS-Pz.Korps*: "*The* Totenkopf *division will immediately begin to withdraw to the southern bank of the Psel with all its heavy weapons and all vehicles which are not indispensable. The division will hold itself ready to evacuate its final elements from the bridgehead on the night between the 17th and 18th*" . On the afternoon of July 16, the first elements of the division began to move to the southern bank of the Psel. At the end of the day, the *Totenkopf* reported that it still had 30 *PzKpfw III*, 27 *PzKpfw IV*, 9 *PzKpfw VI Tiger*, 7 *Befehls-Pz.*, 20 *StuG III* and 3 *Marder II*. On July 17, *II.SS-Pz.Korps* received orders to regroup in the Bjelgorod sector. *SS-Pz.Rgt.3* crossed the Psel again beginning at 22:10. The withdrawal was accompanied by Soviet artillery fire. The decision to abandon the bridgehead threw all of the SS soldiers who had fought and suffered for an entire week into a fit of rage. The last to withdraw were the engineers who mined the entire sector as well as bridges and houses.

A *Totenkopf Tiger*, July 1943.

The *I./"T"* remained as the rear guard and was engaged in combat to slow down the Soviet advance. Its commander, *SS-Hstuf.* Eckert, was wounded during the withdrawal. Around midnight, all of the *Totenkopf* units had crossed to the southern bank of the Psel. At 4:45 on July 18, the *Totenkopf* reported that it had assumed its new positions. The Soviets, however, did not stay idle and in the morning attacked at Gresnoje. They were driven off by heavy weapons fire, but continued to attack despite that. The *SS-Korps-Werfer-Abt.* supported the *Eicke* Regiment in its sector. At 11:00, the Soviets attacked again, this time from the Komsomolez woods, supported by about fifteen tanks. Three *T-70* tanks managed to penetrate the German defenses; two of them were destroyed by a *Pak 38* of *2.Bttr./SS-Korps-Werfer-Abt.* and the third by a direct hit from a *Nebelwerfer* rocket launcher. Around 18:00, as planned, *XLVIII.Pz.Korps* took over the sector of *II.SS-Pz.Korps,* which had been ordered to reach the Stalino area. Meanwhile, *Heeresgruppe Süd* had decided to retire *4.Panzer-Armee* from the front line following Operation *Zitadelle,* because it was now useless to hold a salient south of the Psel. During the night between July 18-19, the *Totenkopf* withdrew to a line that ran from northeast of Teterewino, to the north of Wesselyj and Solotino. On July 20, the *Totenkopf* was ordered to reach the Barwenkowa sector rather than the sector north of Stalino. In the period between July 15-19 the division had suffered 512 killed, 2,118 wounded and 38 missing.

Bibliography

M. Afiero, "3.SS-Pz.Div. Totenkopf - Vol. I: 1939-1943", Associazione Culturale Ritterkreuz
M. Afiero, "The 3rd Waffen-SS Pz.Div. Totenkopf 1939-1943: Vol.1", Schiffer Publishing

SS-Gruppenführer und Generalleutnant der Waffen-SS
Fritz von Scholz
by Antonio Guerra

SS-Standartenführer **Fritz von Scholz.**

Fritz Scholz was born on December 9, 1896 in Pilsen in Bohemia. At the beginning of the Great War, in July 1914, he was called up to serve in the Austro-Hungarian army. He served as an artillery officer initially in the *k.u.k. Feld-Artillerie Regiment 22* and engaged on the Eastern front. In May 1915, Fritz was promoted to Leutnant and transferred to the *k.u.k. Feldhaubitzenregiment 3*, always remaining on the Eastern front. In 1917, Fritz was transferred to the *k.u.k. Feldartillerieregiment 40*, serving on the Italian front, as a communications officer. Fritz's father, *Generalmajor* Ferdinand Scholz, also served in the Austro-Hungarian Army on the Eastern Front. During the fighting in the Rerancze area, northeast of Czernowitz in Bukovina, his actions against the Russians attracted the attention of Emperor Franz Joseph. As a result he was awarded the title of Knight of Rerancze (Edler von Rerancze) and thus his family name changed from Scholz to von Scholz Edler von Rerancze. In November 1917, Fritz was promoted to the rank of *Oberleutnant* and transferred again to *Feld Artillerie Regiment 125*, with which he served until April 1919. During the course of the war, Fritz had received numerous decorations, including the Medal in Austro-Hungarian Gold (*Österreichische Goldenen Tapferkeitsmedaille*) and the War Service Cross in both Silver and Bronze (*Österreichische Militärverdienstkreuz*). After leaving the army in 1919, Fritz had sporadic jobs in Klagenfurt, Munich, Leipzig and in Tyrol. In 1921, he enlisted in the *Oberland Freikorp*, participating in the fighting against dissident communists in Silesia. Subsequently, Fritz was attracted to Adolf Hitler's NSDAP, becoming a great supporter of it and decided to join it's austrian branch on October 8, 1932. Soon after he joined the Austrian SA as a platoon commander, participating in street fighting against the communists in Lutzow and Munich. Forming him in June 1933, he was integrated into *SA Gruppe Nordwest*. This militancy of his in the SA created him many problems with the Austrian authorities and at the end of 1933 he was forced to move permanently to Germany In order to avoid being arrested. He then entered the *Schutzstaffel* (Nr.13 5638) serving in the *SS Osterreichschen Legion* based in Linz. In 1934, he was promoted to the rank of *SS-Untersturmführer* and placed in command of the *5.Kompanie* of *II./SS-Standarte 1*.

In Vienna, Schönbrunn 1940: Fritz von Scholz inspects 2nd Bataillon of Regiment *'Nordland'*.

Fritz von Scholz e l'*SS-Stubaf.* Plöw.

Wiking division

At the beginning of World War II, Fritz von Scholz with the rank of *SS-Sturmbannführer* was in command of the *II.Bataillon* of the *SS-Regiment 'Der Führer'*. Still in command of this battalion he took part in the campaign on the Western Front in 1940, during which he was decorated with both classes of the Iron Cross. At the end of the campaign, Fritz was assigned to command a new formation including Danish and Norwegian volunteers, the *SS-Infanterie-Regiment 'Nordland'* stationed at Klagenfurt in Austria. On January 30, 1941, he was promoted to the rank of *SS-Standartenführer*. The *Nordland* Regiment was attached to the new division of the *Waffen SS* together with the *Germania* Regiment and *Westland*. The unit that was initially supposed to be called *Germania*, instead became the *SS-Division Wiking*. The division did not immediately participate in the campaign on the Eastern Front and only went into action at the end of June 1941 in the Tarnopol area of Galicia. Over the next few months, Fritz von Scholz led the *Nordland* Regiment in the fighting along the Dnieper River and around Dnepropetrovsk. In October 1941, Fritz was promoted to *Oberführer* while retaining command of *Nordland*, which ended the year fighting hard at Rostov-on-Don.

SS-Staf. Fritz von Scholz, with some officers of his staff, Russia 1941.

Von Scholz and SS-Stubaf. Polcwacz.

For his valor in combat Fritz was decorated with the German Cross in Gold on 22 November 1941. In December 1941, *Wiking* was ordered to abandon Rostov and withdraw across the Mius River.

The Knight's Cross

Less than a month later, von Scholz was also granted the Knight's Cross for his excellent conduct during the fighting for Rostov, which was officially granted to him on January 19, 1942. Let us read the proposal written by Felix Steiner:

"... *The personal commitment shown by* SS-Oberführer *von Scholz, during the hard defensive fighting on the Dnjepropetrovsk bridgehead, proved decisive after his regiment arrived on the position and for this he was proposed for the award of the* Ritterkreuz des Eisernen Kreuzes; *von Scholz has already been decorated on 11.29.41 with the* Deutsche Kreuz in Gold. *The course of the fighting was decisively influenced by the action of the* SS-Oberführer *von Scholz who personally carried out the most varied tasks which were von Scholz's* Gefechtsgruppe, *during the clashes that took place from 17. to 11.20.1941, in the northern sector of Rostov, had the task of covering the flank of the armored army and performed very well his task by resisting the heavy enemy attacks. Five Russian Divisions, supported by an armored brigade, took turns, from the evening of 17.11 until noon of 20.11, in uninterrupted mass attacks, always supported by heavy tanks. With a constant and continuous use of assault guns and depth attacks by bombers and fighter planes, the enemy attempted to overwhelm von Scholz's* Gefechtsgruppe, *which responded in a determined and orderly manner to these attacks carried out at various points, along a front sector of no less than 24 kilometres.*

SS-Oberführer **Fritz von Scholz with the** *Ritterkreuz* **and** *SS-Stubaf.* **Walter Plöw, 1941.**

The men of this Gefechtsgruppe *opposed to the concentrated attack by Russian forces of the 37th Army which had begun by striking deep into the flank of 1.Panzerarmee advancing on Rostow. The success of SS-Oberführer von Scholz's* Gefechtsgruppe, *which for four days resisted the attacks of enormously superior forces, would not have been conceivable without the intervention of SS-Oberführer von Scholz, always present on the front line, in the most dangerous sectors both day and night.*

On 18.11, in Dobropolje, even with infantry weapons alone, he opposed the mass attacks carried out by enemy tanks that had broken through behind his positions. He was at the forefront with the men of his III.Bataillon when in the locality of Tuslowo, he had to face and repel the furious attacks

SS-Brigadeführer **Fritz von Scholz.**

SS-Brigdf. **von Scholz decorates Latvian volunteers.**

of the 99th and 253rd Caucasian divisions. While the tanks partially managed to penetrate the defensive line, the Soviet infantry was unable to get close to the men of the SS-Rgt. Nordland. In recent days, through his personal intervention, he has made it possible to block and resolve this moment of crisis, and every evening, he has been able to announce to the Division command that, along his front, all the enemy armored and infantry attacks had been repulsed with heavy losses for the latter.

In the evening of 20.11, the front was re-established despite the uninterrupted enemy assaults carried out with the use of tanks, infantry and assault guns. The enemy was stopped thanks to the steadfastness of this commander who managed to block and then push back an adversary determined to break through the front. In the afternoon of 11.21, the division, employed on an intermediate position, was able to repel new enemy attacks. A rapid advance by Pz.Rgt.2 on Balabanow enabled elements of his Gefechtsgruppe *to capture some four hundred prisoners".*

In the early summer of 1942, with the launch of *Operation Blau* and the advance of Army Group South towards Stalingrad, *Wiking* was once again engaged in the conquest of Rostov and subsequently in the advance towards the Caucasus. Despite the strong resistance put up by the Soviet forces, the units of the division reached the gates of Asia, eventually having to fall back to avoid being trapped. In December 1942, Fritz von Scholz was promoted to the rank of *Brigadeführer*.

Von Scholz decorates Dutch volunteers, 1943.

Spring 1943: von Scholz and Himmler.

New assignments

On January 10, 1943, von Scholz was recalled to Germany to take command of a new SS division still being formed at Grafewöhr. Since the new unit had not yet been fully formed, von Scholz was transferred back to the Eastern Front, first to assume command of the *1.SS-Infanterie-Brigade (mot.)* attached to the Army Group of Center and then of the *2.SS-Infanterie-Brigade (mot.)* attached to Army Group North. On April 20, 1943, von Scholz was recalled to Grafewöhr to assume command of *11.SS-Freiwilligen-Panzergrenadier-Division Nordland.* Wiking's old *Nordland* Regiment had been used as the nucleus for the new formation. The division was initially transferred to Croatia where the SS units were fighting against the communist partisan bands. In January 1944, *Nordland* was transferred to the Leningrad Front along the Oranienbaum Pocket, attached to *Generalfeldmarschall* Walter Model's Army Group North. Von Scholz led the division during the retreat to Narva and during the battles on the bridgehead of the same name. During this campaign he was under the orders of his old commander, *SS-Obergruppenführer* Felix Steiner, commander of the *III.(gemanisches) SS-Panzerkorps* to which *Nordland* was attached. During the defensive battles in the city of Narwa the leadership of Fritz von Scholz had a strong impact on the fighting spirit of his men. Because of his friendly and jovial way of dealing with his men, he was jokingly called *Papa Scholz* or *Alte Fritz* (old Fritz). His visits to the front were frequent and above all he was very concerned about the state of his troops. *Nordland* along with the other

The *SS-Brigdf*. Fritz von Scholz, second from right, at Narva in February 1944.

Fritz von Scholz during the ceremony for the awarding of the Knight's Cross to the *SS-Hstuf*. Heinz Hämel.

Narva front, 1944: from the left, *SS-Stubaf*. Albrecht Krügel, *SS-Gruf*. von Scholz and *SS-Ostubaf*. Fritz Knöchlein.

elements of the *III SS Armored Corps* held their positions for a good five months.

The Oak Leaves

For these actions, Fritz von Scholz was awarded the Oak Leaves for his Knight's Cross on March 12, 1944, again at the suggestion of Felix Steiner. Let's read the text: "....SS-Brigadeführer *Fritz von Scholz fought in the campaign on the Eastern front, in the north-eastern sector and has been engaged hard until today, from 16 January 1944, continuing to command the division, establishing itself for its method of use and combativeness as an example for its troops. Its division has completed the task of blocking the huge enemy forces, preventing their advance along the main Kipen-Narwa road. these heavy and continuous fightings, there have been various moments of crisis, which have always been dominated in an exemplary manner by the personal intervention of the commander of the division.*

1.) On 28.1.1944, the enemy attacked advancing on both sides of the Kipen-Narwa railway line, south of Osertizy, pinning down the remnants of 10.Lw.FD.Div., disarraying 61.I.D. and blocking the railway line needed for westward travel, north of Gurlewo. The Lohmann combat group of the 11.SS-Fr.Pz.Gr.Div. 'Nordland' which was in Osertizy, escaped the danger but in the south the units of 10.Lw.FD.Div. including Div.Stab., have been surrounded by the enemy. The division commander, SS-Brigdf. *Fritz von Scholz, from Ljalizy launched a night counterattack on Gurlewo reaching the railway line and driving the enemy back east, allowing the staff group of 10.Lw.Feld.Div. to take the road towards Ljalizy.*

The *SS-Gruf.* Fritz von Scholz, with his hand bandaged for a wound, during a decoration ceremony for soldiers of the SS *Nordland* division, June 1944.

SS-Brigadeführer **Fritz von Scholz.**

2.) On 1.2.1944, the 11.SS-Freiw.Pz.Gren.Div. she was picked up from Jamburg to Dubrowka. The enemy with numerous forces crossed the front both to the north and to the south and attacked the railway line at that point, clashing with the units of the division. SS-Brigadeführer Fritz von Scholz was the soul of the resistance in the knowledge that what remained of the 61.I.D., 227.I.D. and 10.Lw.Feld.Div., was to fall back west on Narva, even though there was little time to make this move. Despite the repeated and strong attacks, also supported by tanks, the units of the division prevented the impact of the enemies, with the strength of a regiment, from being able to break through the lines. The stubborn resistance, held on both sides of Jamburg, Dubrowka and on the sides of Komarowka, which withstood the attacks of superior enemy forces, created the prerequisite for the orderly occupation of the Narva bridgehead and the regrouping of suitable forces to the occupation of the northern positions of Narva itself. The firmness of the units of the 11.SS-Freiw.Pz.Gren.Div. 'Nordland' *made it possible to gain time to quickly lead the* Panz.Gren.Div. 'Feldherrnhalle' *and further reinforcements, allowing the remnants of* 61. *and* 170.I.D. *and of the* 10.Lw.Feld.Div. *to move orderly in the western sector of Narva. The determination of the forces under the command of* SS-Brigadeführer *Fritz von Scholz created the prerequisite for further fighting on the Narva front, even if the center of gravity and the decisive factors of this front are to be assessed. The personal use and example of the* SS-Brigadeführer *Fritz von Scholz with his severity, have in fact spurred his troops to very high values of heroism. He has once again led the young division, with exemplary strength".*

SS-Gruppenführer **Fritz von Scholz.**

Death on the field

On April 20, 1944, Fritz von Scholz was promoted to the rank of *SS-Gruppenführer*. At the end of July, the units of the III SS Armored Corps moved along a new defensive line west of Narva, the *Tannenbergstellung*, articulated on three hills. On July 27, 1944, around noon, von Scholz went to the command post on Hill 69.9, to confer with those in charge of the position. The meeting was attended by the *SS-Ostubaf.* Albrecht Krügel, commander of the *Danmark* regiment and the *SS-Ustuf.* Herwarth Arera, commander of *1.Kp./SS-Pi.Btl.11*: *"You must send troops to reinforce the defensive line; the situation is serious, but we must continue to hold positions"*, ordered von Scholz to the two officers. After having witnessed the organization of an emergency *Kampfgruppe* placed under the orders of the *SS-Ustuf.* Arera himself, von Scholz went immediately afterwards to inspect the positions of the 13./*Danmark* of the *SS-Hstuf.* Erik Krislian Lärum, to ensure adequate artillery support for the frontline grenadiers. "Old Fritz" as his men affectionately called her, arrived at 13./*Danmark* just as a heavy bombardment by enemy artillery had begun: a howitzer shell exploded a short distance from von Scholz, raising a cloud of smoke and throwing shrapnel in all directions. Just one of these splinters struck von Scholz in the face. His face instantly transformed into a mask of blood. The commander lost consciousness and gave no signs of life, although he was immediately rescued and taken to the Rakvere field hospital. The *SS-Ostubaf.* Franz Riedweg, medical officer of *Nordland* of Swiss origin gave him first aid: *"The cranial trauma is serious, he needs to be operated on urgently at the Weisenberg hospital"*, were his first words. For Riedweg, the old Fritz, was not only a boss but above all a friend, with whom he had shared from the beginning the idea of the European *Waffen SS* and the enlistment of foreign volunteers in the German armed forces.

Another photo of the ceremony for the delivery of the Iron Crosses to *Nordland* soldiers attended by Fritz von Scholz, on the right (U.S. NARA).

Rather than transporting the wounded man in a carriage, the train was preferred: a special carriage was prepared at the Vaivara station, where the *SS-Hstuf.* Heinz Hämel also found a place, who was also wounded the previous day. Throughout the journey, Hämel watched over his commander, whose condition appeared more and more serious by the hour. When the convoy reached Weisenberg, von Scholz had already expired: the commander of the *Nordland* had died of his serious wounds. It was a great loss for the *Nordland* division, the *Waffen-SS* and for all German armed forces.

The Concession of the Swords

Posthumously, on August 8, 1944, von Scholz was awarded the Swords for his Knight's Cross with Oak Leaves, again on a written proposal from Felix Steiner sent to the *Reichsführer-SS* via telex. Let's read the short text: "....*On 7.24.44, the enemy, after a two-hour drumming artillery fire, broke in with the tanks in the sector of the G.R.45, with the center of gravity on both sides of the main road of Lipsu, penetrating to a width of 1 kilometer and a depth of 1 kilometer. The conquest of the adjacent high ground took place because it was essential to be able to continue the advance. SS-Gruppenführer Scholz personally led the troops to the front line creating defense points that prevented the second break of the front.After preparing the positions of 4./SS-Panzer-Abteilung 11, the commander personally led a counterattack with 4./SS-Pz.Abt.11 and the 2./Pi.Kp. on the ground at high altitude, managing to push back the enemy and firmly regain possession of the previous main line of battle. It was a success: the break in the front assumed by the enemy did not take place and the infiltration of the Soviet troops along the Narva road was prevented. The enemy attack by the 120th division, which had the assumptions of expelling the 3.SS-Pz.Korps from the Tannenberg position, ended in nothing*".

Fritz von Scholz (center) with Walter Plöw (left) and an unknown *SS-Untersturmführer*, in Russia 1943.

In memory of von Scholz

We report the text of an article that appeared in the newspaper of the 20th Estonian SS division *'Varemeist SS Touseb Kättemaks'*, dated 29 August 1944, entitled *'The SS-Gruppenführer and Generalleutnant der Waffen-SS Fritz von Scholz has fallen'*: "He was well known by the Estonians. Just a few days ago, before his death, he had visited our troop deployment at the front. As always, where the situation was warmest, he was there, ready to personally gain control of the situation in the front line sector; he was a fiery fighter, with a fatherly heart. He cared particularly for his men from 'Nordland'. The Scandinavians and Germans from the Balkan areas, who belonged to his division, loved their commander like a father. 'Old Fritz has fallen'. Only his humorous eyes are still before us urging us to live. One of the best officers of the Waffen-SS fell as he walked out of our brotherhood, fighting for the freedom of Europe. The Ritterkreuz was awarded on 1.18.1942 and the Oak Leaves on 3.12.1944 in recognition of the heroic fighting that the 'Nordland' division waged on the Narva front. We are aware of the criticality of the clashes of those days and weeks in Narva and how SS-Gruppenführer von Scholz supported these successful fights along the broad front he held. Even in that juncture of retreat fighting, he was always at the front, on the front line, where he was seriously wounded. 23 hours later, on July 28, 1944, the commander of the 'Nordland' dies after having sustained countless battles, having sacrificed his life for the freedom of Europe. On August 2, the III.Germanische SS-Panzerkorps, buried its faithful comrade in the Marienburg heroic cemetery and the event was attended by Generalkommissar Litzmann and SS-Brigadeführer Möller. On behalf of SS-Obergruppenführer Steiner, our division commander, SS-Brigadeführer Ausberger, gave a farewell speech. The officer of our division also placed a wreath on the grave commemorating the fallen of the 20.Estnischen SS-Division, on the Narva front. At the same time the commander of a regiment of the 'Nederland', the SS-Obersturmbannführer Collani, was buried, to whom the Führer awarded the Ritterkreuz after his heroic death. After a life studded with combat, the death of SS-Gruppenführer von Scholz meant that the Führer, on August 8, awarded him the Swords. The Commander of the 'Nordland' rests at the top of the beach of the bay of Reval, in the shadow of this beautiful city of Turmstadt, as an eternal sentinel of his distant homeland. We Estonian SS men are aware that the name of Fritz von Scholz will remain in the heart of the Estonian people forever. His name will go down in history for fighting on the Narva front".

Bibliografia

Massimiliano Afiero, "5.SS-Pz.Div. Wiking, volume 1: 1941-1943", Associazione Culturale Ritterkreuz
Veit Scherzer, "*Die Ritterkreuzträger 1939–1945*", Scherzers Militaer-Verlag.
Mark C. Yerger, "*Waffen-SS Commanders: The Army, Corps and Divisional Leaders of a Legend: Krüger to Zimmermann (v. 2)*", Schiffer Military History

The Italian 8th Army in Russia Summer 1942

by Massimiliano Afiero and Ralph Riccio

General Gabriele Nasci (USSME).

General Italo Gariboldi (USSME).

Ever since the formation of the CSIR in the summer of 1941, the Italian Supreme Command had already begun to plan to expand the Italian expeditionary corps with at least another army corps. This decision had been dictated by Mussolini himself, who was desirous to send a greater number of Italian troops to the Eastern Front to increase the political impact of the undertaking. Nevertheless, it was necessary to wait until the summer of 1942, more precisely until 9 July 1942, when the CSIR headquarters was replaced by headquarters of the Italian 8th Army, commanded by General Italo Gariboldi, consisting in addition to the CSIR (renamed as the XXXV Army Corps), the II Army Corps, commanded by General Giuseppe Zanghieri, consisting of the 2nd 'Sforzesca', 3rd 'Ravenna' and 5th 'Cosseria' divisions and the Alpine Army Corps, led by General Gabriele Nasci, consisting of the 2nd 'Tridentina', 3rd 'Julia' and 4th 'Cuneense' alpine divisions. Units directly subordinate to the corps were the 156th Infantry Division 'Vicenza', the horse-mounted grouping (two cavalry regiments and a horse-drawn artillery regiment), the army artillery grouping, engineer units, infantry units, the chemical group, air units (an observation group and a fighter group) and the Croat Legion. The presence of Militia units was also notably increased, with the formation of two raggruppamenti, directly subordinate to II and XXXV Army Corps. In particular, subordinate to II Corps, was the Raggruppamento CC.NN. '23 Marzo', commanded by Lieutenant General Enrico Francisci, consisting of the CC.NN. 'Valle Scrivia' Battalion Grouping (V and XXXIV CC.NN. battalions and the XLI CC.NN. Support Weapons Battalion) and the CC.NN. 'Leonessa' Battalion Grouping (XIV and XV CC.NN. battalions and the XXXVIII CC.NN. Support Weapons Battalion).

General Italo Gariboldi, commander of the Italian army in Russia (ARMIR), reviewing troops at the Stalino (Donetz) airfield in June 1942. (USSME)

General Messe reviewing troops, 1942.

Subordinate to the XXXV Army Corps was the Raggruppamento CC.NN. '3 gennaio', under Lieutenant General Filippo Diamanti, consisting of the CC.NN. Battalion Grouping 'Tagliamento' (LXII and LXXIX CC.NN. battalions and the LXIII CC.NN. Support Weapons Battalion) and the CC.NN.Battalion Grouping 'Montebello' (VI and XXX CC.NN. battalions and XII CC.NN. Support Weapons battalion).

These two ragruppamenti were in reality two small divisions, lighter than army divisions, but better armed and trained. With the transformation of the 63rd Legion into Battalion Groupings, Console Niccolò Nichiarelli was promoted and left the command to

Console Domenico Mittica.

Soldiers of the Tagliamento Blackshirt Legion, Summer 1942 (USSME).

Italian soldiers on the Eastern Front, 1942 (USSME).

Unit Transfer

The departure of new units of the Italian army began in the first week of June and it was established that the Alpine Army Corps would be the last to leave. The German headquarters had designated the area southwest of Kharkov as an unloading and assembly area for II Army Corps, while for the Alpine Army Corps the area north of Taganrog had been chosen. The Italian Supreme Command quickly made it clear that the 8th Army was to be employed in a cohesive manner, without subdividing its forces, as had already happened with the CSIR. Between 17 June and 7 July, a large portion of II Corps units reached the area of Kharkov, including the headquarters with most of its directly subordinated units, the entire 'Ravenna' Division and half of the 'Sforzesca'. Shortly afterwards, the order was given to move the troops towards the Donets, to approach the XXXV Corps operational area and to begin to assemble the

Army.

Bersaglieri on the Eastern Front during a ceremony, Summer 1942 (USSME).

Bersaglieri motorcyclist during a recon mission, 1942.

While the move of new units arriving from Italy was being completed, in light of the resumption of the offensive, the Army commander decided to reinforce the XXXV Corps artillery groups, which since 3 June had been subordinated to 17.Armee, because they were already on the line and about to be committed to combat once again. In addition, also transferred to the same corps was the 'Sforzesca' Division, which had just arrived from Italy, which replaced the 'Torino'. The cavalry raggruppamento and the 'Monte Cervino' alpine ski battalion fell under direct subordination of the Army headquarters. The Alpine Army Corps was still in Italy.

New German summer offensive

German plans for the summer of 1942 were focused mainly on the southern sector of the Eastern Front. Attacks against Moscow or Leningrad were temporarily put off until a later date. For the prosecution of the war, which by now had become worldwide with involvement of Japan and the United States, the Third Reich was urgently in need of raw materials and oil. The objectives of the new offensive, code named Fall Blau (Case Blue), defined by Hitler in Directive Number 41 dated 5 April 1942, called for wiping out the Soviet forces located between the Donets Basin and the Don, the conquest of the passes in the Caucasus and seizure of the rich oil fields on the Caspian Sea.

Resumption of German operations, July-November 1942 (USSME).

There was also another objective, much more ambitious, which was a linkup of the Italo-German forces from Egypt with Japanese forces from India, in order to directly strike at British interests in the Middle East and in Asia Minor. The offensive, which was to involve Army Group South exclusively, had been subdivided into four distinct operational phases: initially the enemy defensive line on the Don at Voronezh (*Blau 1*), then conquer the entire Don Basin as far as the Donets (*Blau 2*). Soon after, German forces were to be engaged in the conquest of the entire area between the Don, Stalingrad and Rostov (*Blau 3*). At that point the offensive was to shift to the south with the objective of conquering the entire Caucasus region, including the areas between the Caspian Sea, the Black Sea and the Volga and the mountainous chain of the Caucasus, with its rich oil deposits (*Blau 4*).

Waffen-SS infantry and armour advancing, Summer 1942 (*Bundesarchiv*).

General Erich von Manstein in 1938.

Prior to launching this new offensive, the Germans were engaged in eliminating several dangerous Soviet salients which were wedged along the German front, at Kharkov, Izyum and the Kerch peninsula. In early May, Soviet forces had launched an offensive in the Izyum area but were surrounded and completely wiped out, losing more than a thousand tanks and 2,500 guns, as well as more than 240,000 men taken prisoner, not counting dead and wounded. On the Crimean front, the German 11th Army under General von Manstein was able to conquer the entire peninsula. Between 10 and 26 June, other offensive actions were mounted with which the Germans established a bridgehead on the eastern bank of the Donets River to the east of Kharkov. These moves made it possible to establish the departure points for the new offensive. Case Blue began officially on 28 June and from the earliest clashes it seemed that the rapid advances of the preceding summer were being repeated, with the Germans attacking and the Soviets being overrun or forced to withdraw. The first forces to move were those deployed in the Voronezh sector and at the beginning of July German armored thrusts crossed the Don.

Bersaglieri during an attack on the Eastern Front, July 1942 (USSME).

German troops and a Sd.Kfz. 251 armored half-track.

This time, however, the Soviets withdrew in time, along a new defensive line further to the east. This sudden withdrawal avoided the loss of major forces but most of all forced the Germans to continue the offensive along two different axes, with the resultant separation of the forces involved. On 9 July Army Group South was split into two new Army Groups: Army Group A, under Marshal Wilhelm List, and Army Group B, under Marshal von Weichs. Army Group A consisted of Ruoth's 1.Armee, Hoth's 4.Panzer-Armee and von Kleist's 1.Panzer-Armee. Army Group B consisted of von Salmuth's 2.Armee, 6.Armee under Paulus, the Romanian 3rd and 4th Armies, the Italian 8th Army and the Hungarian 2nd Army. Hitler's new directive, Number 43 dated 23 July 1942, fixed the objectives of the German offensive along two very distinct routes: Army Group B was to rapidly seize Stalingrad (Operation Fischereiher: Heron) and secure the left flank of Army Group A which was to push to the Caucasus (Operation Edelweiss: Alpine Star).

Italian artillery in action, summer 1942. (USSME)

Occupation of the Krasny Lutsch mineral basin

According to agreements established between the Italian and German headquarters, while awaiting the assembly of all of the 8th Army's units, it had been decided to initially commit to combat only the XXXV Army corps, subordinate to 17.Armee, for the new summer offensive. As previously mentioned, the corps had been reinforced with the 'Sforzesca' Division and with 111.Infanterie-Division, in addition to receiving strong artillery support in view of its action on the Donets front. The corps also received the cavalry raggruppamento and the 'Monte Cervino' alpine ski battalion as reinforcements.

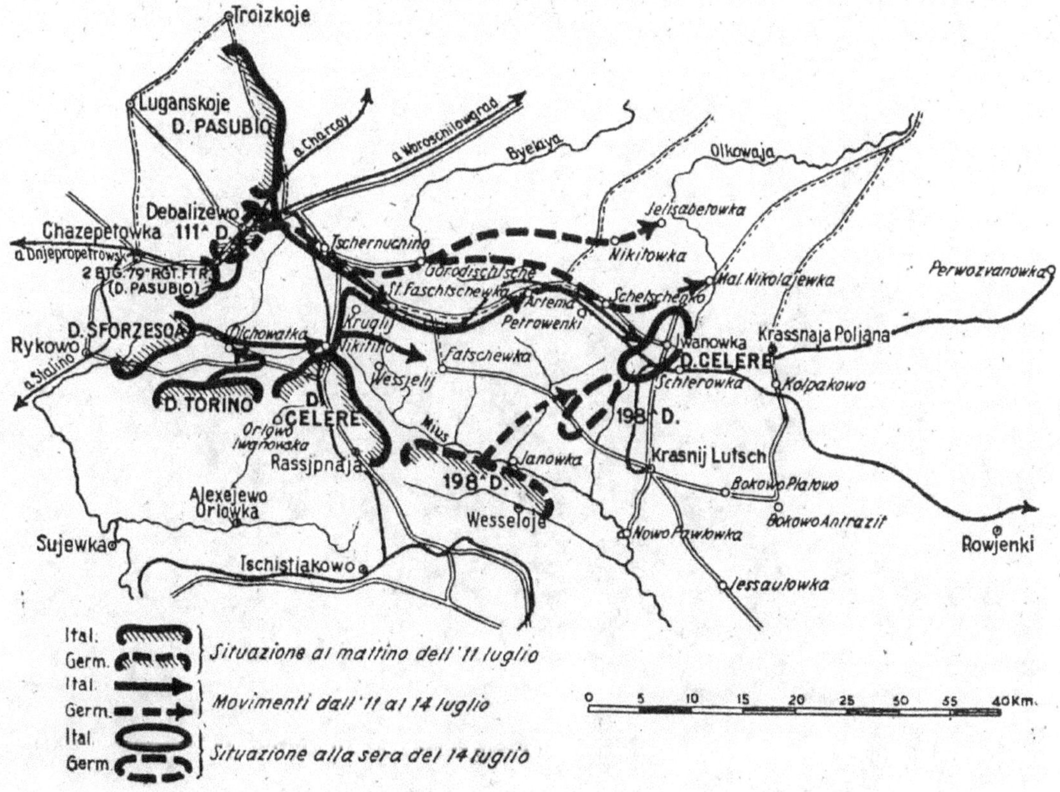

Operations for the conquest of the Krasny Lutsch mineral basin, 11-14 July 1942. (USSME)

Colonel Umberto Salvatores.

The so-called Krasny Lutsch maneuver, carried out between 11 and 22 July, developed in three phases:

1) Initially, the Soviet front between Debalzevo and Nikitino was to be broken with the CC.NN. Battalion Grouping 'Tagliamento', with a converging action by 'Pasubio' and the 111.Infanterie-Division from the north and by the 'Celere', the 'Sforzesca' and the horse-mounted raggruppamento from the south, towards the Fatschevka station, then proceeding to Ivanovka, which had been abandoned following the Christmas Battle.

2) Having reached Ivanovka, the Soviet defensive line between Voroshilovgrad [now Luhnask] and Krasny Lutsch was to be eliminated.

3) Finally, it was necessary to make an encircling move around all of the Soviet forces present in the Krasny Lutsch-Bokovo Pitovo-Bokova Antrazit area.

An Italian defensive position with an antitank gun, summer 1942. (USSME)

During the morning of 11 July, the 'Celere' Division headquarters sent out two reconnaissance in force detachments, the first conducted by the Croat Legion on the ridge of Hill 253.4 towards Vessieli and the second by the LXII CC.NN. Battalion (of the 'Tagliamento' group) toward the town of Nikitino, with the aim of stabilizing the situation on the ground and overrunning the enemy's forward positions, stabilizing the departure points for the attacks that were to follow.

Bersaglieri during an attack, Summer 1942. (USSME)

A flamethrower in action during an attack.

The two recons, adequately supported by divisional artillery, were successful and by nightfall orders for an offensive action were issued. At dawn on 12 July, the 3rd Bersaglieri Regiment, reinforced by the 3rd Bersaglieri Motorcycle Company and a 75/27 group of the 120th Artillery Regiment, after having left Nikitino and Vassieli in the hands of the forces that had occupied them the day before, advanced in two columns: on the left the XX Battalion and the 3rd Motorcycle Company moved towards the station at Fatschevka and on the right the XVII Battalion advanced towards Hill 333.5 (Mogila Ostraya). The rest of the division followed close behind in four echelons in the two directions cited. A sudden storm hampered the movement of the motor vehicles and slowed the advance of the troops, who at the same time were engaged in overcoming enemy resistance that had been left as rear guards, as well as many minefields.

Bersaglieri motorcyclists on a recon mission, summer 1942. (USSME)

General Messe reviewing Italian troops.

At 18:00, the division commander ordered a new column, designated the Salvatores column, led by Colonel Umberto Salvatores, consisting of the VI Bersaglieri Battalion of the 6th Regiment, the XLVII Bersaglieri Motorcycle Battalion and a 100/17 group of the 120th Artillery to march on Petrovenki, leapfrogging the 3rd Bersaglieri force. Some hours later, this new column was stalled by strong enemy resistance near the crossroads at Artema. In the event, contact was made with German units on the flanks, in particular on the left at Utkino with Inf.Rgt. 308 (111.Inf.Div.) and on the right with Inf.Rgt. 217 (198.Inf.Div). On the morning of 13 July, General Messe, following the *17.Armee* plan, ordered the *'Celere'* Division to attack Scevschenko-Malaya Nikolaevka and Ivanovka-Krasnaya Polyana to prevent the Soviets from withdrawing and to set up in defensive positions along the Voroshilovgrad-Krasny Lutsch line.

An Alpini mortar crew in action, Summer 1942. (USSME)

Bersaglieri during an attack, Summer 1942.

At the same time, the 'Pasubio' and 'Sforzesca' divisions, in the second echelon, were to follow the movement to the east. Thus, the 'Celere' commander, General Mario Marazzani, ordered the Salvatores column to eliminate Soviet resistance at the Artema crossroads, occupy the Petrovenki railway station and continue on to Krasnaya Polyana. The recon patrols that had been sent ahead reported that the Sveschenko position on the left was strongly defended while on the right, near Hill 367.1, the Soviet rearguards had stalled the advance of 198.Inf.Div. The division commander, Generalmajor Albert Buck, thus requested aid from Italian units and the VI Bersaglieri Battalion attacked and took the hill.

Towards evening, the bulk of the 'Celere' formed into two columns near the Kommendantski railway station. During the night, Soviet cavalry units supported by artillery and mortars, attacked Hill 367.1; the Italians counterattacked and pushed back the Soviets who left many dead and wounded on the field.

A Monte Cervino mortar crew in action, Summer 1942. (USSME)

A 20mm Breda antiaircraft gun in action, 1942.

At dawn on 14 July, the attacks resumed; troops of the German 111.Inf.Div. attacked towards Yelisabetovka and Malaya Nikolaievka, while the 'Pasubio' was ordered to take up positions between the 111.Inf.Div. and the 'Celere'. At 3:30, the VI Bersaglieri Battalion, supported by III horse artillery group, with the aid of dusk, made a surprise attack against Hill 360.2, a vital position needed for the advance against Ivanovka. After half an hour of fighting the hill was taken and more than 200 prisoners were captured in addition to a large quantity of equipment. At 6:00 all of the units moved forward and were soon challenged by Soviet infantry supported by artillery, mortar and Katyusha rocket launchers. To overcome the stiff enemy resistance, intervention by the Luftwaffe was requested; due to an error, at least initially, the Stuka dive bombers hit the Italian columns, causing several wounded. Later, the Stukas hit the Soviet positions.

Bersaglieri during a rare break in the fighting, Summer 1942. (USSME)

Horse cavalry group marching, Summer 1942. (USSME)

Between 8:00 and 9:00, Ivanovka was captured following furious house-to-house fighting. The Soviets pulled back to the heights to the east of the village, continuing to hit the position with their artillery.

On the XXXV Corps left wing, the 111.Inf.Div. occupied Malaya Nikolaievka, while on the right wing, 198.Inf.Div. was stalled in its attack, leaving the right flank of XXXV Corps exposed. General Messe ordered the horse cavalry group to provide cover. Initially, the 'Celere' headquarters had sent the 'Tagliamento' group and the Croat Legion to the sector previously occupied by the 198.Inf.Div. These two units stayed to defend the positions of the German division and were integrated into the 'Pasubio' Division. Between 15 and 16 July, all unit moves were suspended so that XXXV Corps would be able to reorganize its units. It was planned to deploy the 'Pasubio' and 'Sforzesca' in the area between the 'Celere' and 198.Inf.Div. on 17 July, while the units that has replaced the German division were to remain in the positions that they had occupied.

A Black Shirt machine gun team with a Breda Model 30 during an attack, summer 1940. The soldier on the right has an ammunition chest and two spare barrels on his back. (USSME)

Black Shirts in an attack, summer 1942. (USSME)

At 7:00 on 17 July, responsibility for the Krasny Lutsch sector was assigned to the 'Sforzesca' Division. This freed the 'Celere' to be used to exploit its success. Throughout the day of 17 July, recon patrols continued to meet with stiff enemy resistance. In the 111.Inf.Div. sector there was a tank attack that was repulsed.

Black Shirts attack

On the morning of 17 July, the LXXIX 'M' Battalion had been ordered to carry out a recon mission and to take the village of Shterovka and Hill 342. Thus, at 11:00 in the morning, without any preparatory artillery fire so as not to alert the Soviet defenders, two recon squads led by capomanipolo [Lieutenant] Mario Zago moved towards Shterovka. After having gone about 500 meters, the Black Shirts came under fire from automatic weapons and mortars. Italian artillery quickly came into action in an attempt to ease the pressure, while the Black Shirts of the 2nd Company of Centurione [Captain] Rota moved forward in support of Zago's patrols. The offensive action thus was able to continue and the legionnaires reached the outlying houses of Shterovka, where Soviet riflemen were entrenched and supported by numerous machine gun positions.

A section of Brixia mortars manned by Black Shirts supporting an attack, summer 1942. The officer on the left is armed with a Beretta MAB 38A submachine gun. (USSME)

A Breda Model 30 in action against enemy positions.

Among the first to fall to enemy fire was Lieutenant Zago, along with other Black Shirts. The officer lay on the ground, badly wounded. It was in that moment that one of his Black Shirts, Mario Paolucci, having seen his commanding officer wounded on the ground, brought himself closer to save him. In the morning he had already been wounded in his right arm, but had taken part in the attack by pulling ammunition chests along with his other arm. When Paoloucci approached the officer on the ground, a burst from a Soviet machine gun wounded him in the left arm. Finding it impossible to drag Zago with either arm, despite the pain, Paolucci decided to grab his commander's jacket with his teeth, managing to drag his body for a long stretch, until he was

in World War Two 1939-1945

once again hit in the chest by enemy fire and dying.

Black Shirts in an attack, summer 1942. (USSME)

Mario Paolucci (MOVM).

He was the Legion's first recipient of the Gold Medal for Military Valor, with the following citation: *'Unable to wait, even though he was a retired officer, he enlisted as a simple soldier. Always a volunteer for the riskiest actions, during violent fighting, he went on the attack against well-fortified positions using hand grenades, an example to all of his fellow soldiers. Seriously wounded in his right arm, he did not desist from the action, continuing to fight with lion-like courage. Having reached the enemy position and during a violent counterattack, because ammunition was running out, he crossed the area under fire bringing several ammunition chests with him using only his left arm. Seeing his officer fall, while enemy reaction became increasingly furious, he quickly went to him to offer aid. Hit by a machine gun burst which immobilized his left arm as well, he dragged himself to his officer and, seizing part of his jacket with his teeth, with supreme effort was able to drag him for a short stretch until, mortally wounded, he consecrated his indomitable heroism on the field of battle'.*
[Shterovka, Russian Front, 17 July 1942].

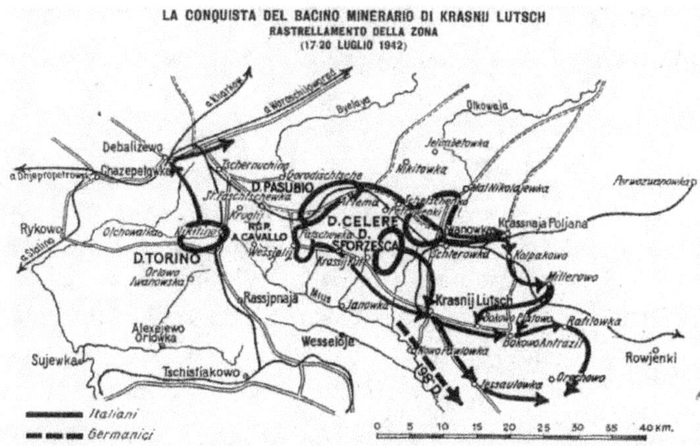

Operations for the conquest of the Krasny Lutsch mineral basin; sweep of the area (17-20 July 1942).

The Black Shirts of the 2nd Company also suffered some losses. At 13:00 Console [Colonel] Mittica ordered all the recon patrols to return, which withdrew bringing their wounded and all of their equipment along with them. During the withdrawal the 2nd Company commander, Captain Rota, was also wounded. All of the other officers of the company were also wounded. Shortly after, the Soviets attacked, exerting maximum effort against the 1st Company's positions. The men of the 2nd Company went to its aid, led by Centurione Alberto Mingiardi, and those of the 3rd Company, led by Seniore [Major] Silvio Margini. The Soviet riflemen were forced to withdraw and during the night they abandoned the entire sector. On the morning of the following day, under a driving rain, the legionnaires of the LXXIX 'M' Battalion captured Shterovka first and then Surayevka, capturing two hundred prisoners and a large amount of arms and munitions.

New orders

The next day, Heeresgruppe A headquarters issued an order to XXXV Corps to attack the positions at Krasnaya Polyana and Rovenki. These two objectives were assigned respectively to the 'Pasubio' and the 'Celere', while the 'Sforzesca' was to advance on Bokovo Platovo. The horse raggruppamennto was to approach the industrial center of Krasny Lutsch from the south and also aim for Bokovo Platovo. At that time, the bulk of the Soviet forces were pulling back towards the Donets, leaving strong rear guards behind. On 18 July, movement continued to be slowed down by bad weather conditions. The 111.Inf.Div. was subordinated to III.Armee-Korps. The 'Celere' division occupied Shterovka, Kolpakovo and Krasnaya Polyana, where the 'Pasubio' arrived in the evening. After having passed through Krustaliny, the 'Sforzesca' continued on to Hill 347, north of Krasny Lutsch. After an exhausting 60-kilometer march slowed down by mud and minefields, the horse raggruppamento reached the Krasny Lutsch area. Towards evening, the German headquarters ordered XXXV Corps to assemble at Bokovo Platovo to sweep the entire mining area. Between 19 and 22 July, the troops were engaged in these sweeps, capturing about 4,000 prisoners.

On 23 July, 8th Army headquarters, which had become operational, ordered XXXV Corps to move to Luganskaya on the Donets River, near Voroshilovgrad.

Bibliography

Massimilano Afiero & Ralph Riccio, "*Snow, Ice and Sacrifice. The Italian Army in Russia 1941-1943*", Helion & Company Limited

Swedish volunteers in the Waffen-SS

By Sergio Volpe

Birger Furugård.

Konrad Hellgren, Chief of SFKO.

As had already happened in the First World War, also in the Second, Sweden declared itself neutral. During the Winter War, between Finland and Russia, Sweden declared itself 'non-belligerent', in order to be able to support the friendly and neighboring nation. Military aid, in arms, ammunition and volunteers, were sent to the Finns until 13 March 1940, when hostilities ceased. Even when the Germans invaded Denmark and Norway, Sweden continued to remain neutral. In June 1941, with the start of Operation *Barbarossa*, Germany asked the Swedish government for an alignment with the Axis powers, authorizing the transport of men and weapons through Sweden for the Finnish front. After a few days of hesitation, known to history as the *'Midsummer Crisis'*, the Swedish government authorized the passage of the *163.Infanterie-Division* by train towards the Finnish front. However, the state of neutrality was not accepted by all Swedish citizens: many were against their government's policy and voluntarily decided to participate in the civil war in Spain alongside Franco's nationalist forces, in the Finno-Soviet war of 1939-1940 at alongside the Finns and the crusade against Bolshevism alongside the Axis forces.

Even in neutral Sweden, extreme right-wing parties had arisen since the 1920s, following the European nationalist wave. Sweden's first National Socialist movement, *Svenska Nationalsocialistiska Frihetsförbundet*, the Swedish Federation for National Socialist Freedom, was formed on August 12, 1924 by brothers Gunnar, Sigurd and Birger Furugård. Between 1925 and 1926, the activity of this movement manifested itself only in the publication of the weekly "*Nationalsocialisten*" (the National Socialist). In 1929, the movement transformed into the *Svenska Nationalsocialistiska Bonde-och Arbetarpartiet* (National Socialist Swedish Peasants' and Workers' Federation). In 1926, the *Sveriges Fascistika Kampfororganization* (SKFO), the Swedish Fascist Combat Organization, was created in Stockholm by Konrad Hellgren.

Swedish nationalists during a demonstration organized in the 1930s.

Sven-Olof Lindholm.

Hellgren had fought as a volunteer in the Great War and then enlisted in the anti-communist Frankish Corps. Joining him were Lieutenant Sven Hedengren, another Great War veteran, and Sergeant Sven-Olof Lindholm. The Organization published a weekly *'Spöknippet'* (the Fascio), full of anti-Semitic and anti-Communist articles. The symbol of the party was the swastika and its members wore black shirts. In the autumn of 1928, the movement became the *Sveriges Fascistiska Folkparti*, the Swedish Fascist People's Party, and its members began wearing brown shirts.

In 1930, an attempt was made to bring together all the different Swedish fascist and National Socialist groups into one, with the formation of *Nysvenska Nationalsocialistiska Förbundet*, the Swedish National Socialist Renewal Party. But due to conflicts between the different groups, the attempt failed. And so, in early 1931, the *Nysvenska Nationalsocialistiska Förbundet* became the *Svenska Nationalsocialistiska Partiet*, the National Socialist Party of Sweden, under the leadership of Birger Furugård. Starting in 1932, the party expanded reaching about three thousand militants and participating in elections in the country, although obtaining poor results.

Rally of Lindholm party members, 1935.

Sven-Olof Lindholm in uniform.

Among the main representatives of the party, was Sven-Olof Lindholm, former member of the SKFO who had in the meantime abandoned his military career to devote himself totally to politics and to National Socialism. In 1932, conflicts began to arise between Lindholm and Furugård, due to ideological differences. Lindholm's followers were for a more socialist and less conservative National Socialism. In January 1933, during the party congress, Lindholm and his family were expelled from the party and a few weeks later, they founded the Swedish National Socialist Workers' Party (*Nationalsocialistiska Arbetarparti* or NSAP), based in Gothenburg, which immediately met with great support, above all within the Swedish youth. However, internal conflicts also continued in the new movement. In the autumn of 1933, a new party was founded, the National Socialist Bloc, led by Martin Ekström, which again set out to unite all Swedish National Socialist movements. To support this project, Count Eric von Rosen, Göring's son-in-law and veteran of the Finnish War of Independence in 1918. Between 1933 and 1936, Lindholm's party continued to gain support, despite constant disagreements with the other Swedish National Socialist parties.

Sven-Olof Lindholm during a Svensk Socialistisk Samling rally in 1942. Note the party crest in front of the podium.

Swedish Volunteer Corps **skiers on the Finnish front, 1940.**

In 1938, the party changed its name, becoming the Swedish Socialist Union, *Svensk Socialistisk Samling* or SSS. The use of the swastika (in favor of the *Vasakärven*, the coat of arms of the Vasa dynasty), the outstretched salute and the use of uniforms were abandoned, to avoid passing off the movement as a copy of the German National Socialist Party. However, the ideology of the Swedish Nationalist Party remained the same, based on the principles of anti-capitalism, anti-communism and anti-Semitism. During the Second World War, some members of the Swedish party enlisted in the *Frontmannaföreningen Sveaborg*, an association of Swedish volunteers, to fight in the continuation war in Finland. Others instead opted for the *Waffen-SS*.

Young volunteers at one *Waffen-SS* recruiting office.

SS-Ogruf. Berger during a visit at the Sennheim camp.

Swedish volunteers in the Waffen-SS

Since the summer of 1940, the *SS-Brigdf.* Gottlob Berger and *Reichsführer-SS* Himmler began discussions about the possible recruitment of Swedish volunteers into the *Nordland* regiment. Given the country's neutral status, no recruiting offices could be opened in Sweden. On September 4, 1940, Himmler authorized recruitment in Sweden, however diplomatic arrangements had to be made through the Foreign Office. German diplomats (particularly members of the German embassy in Sweden) were not very interested in the project and initially the results were poor. In the following months, some Swedish volunteers crossed the Norwegian border on their own initiative and reported to the SS recruiting office in Oslo.

Berger charged the *SS-Staf.* Paul Dahm, head of *Ergänzungsstelle Nord* (the SS recruiting office in Oslo), to recruit Swedish volunteers. Dahm had already been engaged since February 1941 in the recruitment of Finnish volunteers for the *Waffen-SS*. Precisely during a trip to Finland, Dahm stayed two days in the Swedish capital, where he had talks with German representatives, the German ambassador in Stockholm, Prince of Wied and the members of the Ausland Organisation, the section of the National Socialist Party abroad (which brought together German citizens residing in Sweden), in particular Doctor

Stengl. The latter showed himself to be very interested in the recruitment of Swedish volunteers, placing himself at the disposal of the SS for the creation of a clandestine network, which would have brought the volunteers to the Reich through Norway.

Waffen SS recruiting office in Amsterdam, Holland 1941.

Waffen-SS volunteers during training, Summer 1941.

With the start of Operation *Barbarossa* in June 1941, things changed radically. German propaganda was able to transform this new military campaign into a real crusade of European civilization against Bolshevism, against Stalinist tyranny, in the hope of recruiting many volunteers throughout Europe, including Sweden. The Swedish government received numerous offers to participate directly or indirectly in the war against the Soviet Union. But the Swedes only released volunteers for the Finnish front, they did not officially allow for conscription into the German armed forces. And in the end, the Swedish government itself only allowed the transit of German troops on its national territory. There were ongoing talks to try to get the Swedish government to allow its citizens to move freely to Germany.

Himmler and *Waffen-SS* volunteers.

Clandestine recruitments

After the failure of any possibility of being able to recruit volunteers in Swedish territory, the SS commands were convinced that only clandestine enlistments could be used. Contacts were therefore made with people who could encourage these enlistments, initially Oskar Nordenstein, a Swedish entrepreneur and later Carl Olov Wrang, a veteran of the Finnish-Soviet war. Meanwhile, individual conscriptions of Swedish nationals continued at SS recruiting offices in Norway, Finland and Denmark. After the work done by Dahm, it was decided to assign the delegation of the Germanische Leitstelle (the German liaison office) in Oslo, the task of coordinating the recruitment of volunteers from Sweden.

SS-Stubaf. **Karl Leib, second from the right, during a ceremony at Oslo in 1942, with Vidkun Quisling and others Norwegian personalities (*Riksarkivet*).**

At the head of it was the *SS-Stubaf.* Karl Leib, transferred to Oslo in May 1942, after having headed the same recruiting office in the Netherlands. Leib made frequent trips to Sweden from his base in Oslo, despite the protests of German embassy diplomats, who feared that these clandestine recruitments could jeopardize relations with the Swedish government. But Leib and his collaborators continued their work to recover the largest number of Swedish volunteers.

SS-Ustuf. **Heino Meyer.**

SS-Ustuf. **Gösta Borg.**

The first volunteers that the underground organization in Sweden managed to transfer to Finland arrived in Torneå, on the border with Sweden, in early August. There, they found members of the *Waffen-SS* waiting for them, who after a quick medical examination, embarked them from the port of Vasa with destination Stralsund and then Stettin. As of 1 September 1941, there were 16 Swedish volunteers accommodated in an SS barracks. In that same summer of 1941, other volunteers arrived in Germany, having passed through Norway: among them, Heino Meyer[1], Hans Linden, Fred Nilsson, Gösta Borg[2]. After reporting to the SS Recruiting Office in Oslo, they were given SS uniforms and given papers to be transferred to Germany. Since most of them had already fought as veterans of the Winter War in Finland or as members of the Swedish army, they received minimal training to adapt to German regulation and discipline, before being transferred to the Sennheim training camp in Alsace. Here, the *Waffen-SS* had created a special barracks where non-German volunteers received the necessary pre-military education on the German language, National Socialist ideology, rules and regulations of the German army and above all lots of sporting activity. In Sennheim, volunteers were not trained in the use of weapons. But not all volunteers passed through Sennheim. For example, the group led by the Swedish count Ulph Hamilton was sent directly to the Klagenfurt camp in Austria, where there was the reinforcement battalion of the SS 'Westland' regiment. In September 1941, there were about ten Swedish volunteers in the 4th company of the battalion. In the other companies there were another dozen. This first group of volunteers finished their training in November 1941 and was sent directly to the front in the Ukraine with the SS *Wiking* division. The second group of volunteers, while staying in Klagenfurt in December 1941, took part in anti-partisan operations in the Slovenian mountains. There were no major clashes with the Slavic partisans, however a Swedish volunteer, Sten Olofsson, was seriously wounded in the foot and was discharged. The rest were sent to the *Wiking* division.

Waffen-SS volunteers during training at Sennheim camp, 1941.

A group of Swedish volunteers traveling by sea on a military vessel, from Finland to Germany (*Erik Norling*).

Swedish volunteers in the Wiking

The first Swedish volunteers enrolled in the *Waffen-SS* were transferred to the front line on the Eastern front, with the *Wiking* division. In August 1941, according to the report of the *SS-Gruf.* Berger sent to Himmler about the number of non-German volunteers in the division, only one Swedish volunteer appears. It was *SS-Sturmmann* Ingemar Johansson, a young man of only sixteen, born in October 1925 in Kisa. Before the war he had moved with his family to Prague, where he began working as an apprentice in Skoda industries, only to report to the SS recruiting office, lying about his age. In September 1941, there were at least eight Swedish volunteers. In February 1942, the training group in Klagenfurt joined the division, so that the number of Swedish volunteers in the division reached a total of 25-30. Among these early volunteers were Heino Meyer, Bengt Ohlsson and others. In the *Nordland* regiment there were Tor Samuelsson, Sten Olsson, Nils Eriksson. In *Westland* were Kurt Lundin, Erik Dahlin, Lars Forsberg, Folke Nystrand, Fred Nilsson

SS-Sturmmann **Hans Linden.**

Soldiers of the 4.*Kompanie*/*Westland* in training.

and others. In *1.Kp./Germania* there were Gösta Borg, Bengt Rosmark and Ragnar Linnér. On December 30, 1941, *SS-Sturmmann* Hans Linden, who was serving in *1.Bttr./SS-Flak-Abt.*, died in combat. He was born on 10 September 1922 in Stockholm, immediately an active militant of the youth section of *Svensk Socialistisk Samling*. At 17 he enlisted to fight in Finland against the Soviets, serving in an artillery unit. He later enlisted in the Waffen-SS before the war started in the East: in March 1941, he crossed the Norwegian border together with his friend Fred Nilsson. After training in Graz and Heuberg, due to his experience as a gunner, he was assigned to the anti-aircraft unit of *Wiking*, training in Weimar. After being wounded in combat, Linden contracted dysentery due to poor sanitation at the front and died in the Jusovka field hospital. He was posthumously decorated with the Iron Cross Second Class. In Sweden, the National Socialist party, the Svensk Socialistisk Samling, paid tribute to the young militant who fell in Russia for propaganda purposes.

Linden was presented to the youth members as an example of the ultimate sacrifice. The party newspaper, *'Den Svenke'*, thus announced the loss of Linden[3]: "...*Another fighter has been snatched from our ranks. The head of the Nordisk Ungdom circle, Hans Waldemar Linden, suffered the death of heroes in combat against the Bolshevik world enemy*". On March 30, 1942, another SSS militant, Lars Forssberg, who was serving in *1.Kp./Westland* as a private, died in the Augsburg hospital. He was seriously wounded in combat on December 27, 1941. During the subsequent campaign in the Caucasus, in the summer of 1942, more Swedish volunteers were killed in combat.

Young *Wiking* soldiers on the Eastern front (US. NARA).

Among them was *SS-Schütze* Erik Dahlin, who served in the *Westland* regiment. Dahlin, who comes from a working-class family, initially served in the merchant marine. Then in 1939, he had gone off to volunteer in the Swedish Volunteer Corps for the Winter War. Returning from the Finnish front, he returned to serve in the navy. When his ship was torpedoed by a British submarine in the English Channel in the autumn of 1940, he decided to enlist in the *Waffen-SS*. This happened in the summer of 1941. Dahlin fell in combat at Yegorlyskaya in August 1942. After the retreat from the Caucasus, in the spring of 1943 the *Nordland* regiment and other elements of the division were transferred to the newly formed SS division, which was to be placed in Felix Steiner's *III.(Germ.)SS-Pz.Korps*, the *Nordland* division. Most of *Wiking*'s Scandinavian volunteers were therefore transferred to this new division, which was mainly formed with Danish and Norwegian volunteers, although some chose to stay on. According to official sources there were at least five, but in reality there were about fifteen[4], who continued to serve in the *Wiking* until the end of the war.

(To be continued)

Notes

[1] Heino Meyer was born on July 7, 1923 in Stockholm. He volunteered for the *Waffen-SS* in 1941 and after completing his education, served in the SS *'Wiking'* division. Assigned to *9.Kp.* of the *SS-Inf. Rgt. 'Germania'*, he participated in the German summer offensive in the Caucasus in the summer of 1942. In 1943, Meyer was admitted to the *SS-Junkerschule* in Bad Tölz to become an officer. Promoted to the rank of *SS-Untersturmführer* he was assigned as a platoon commander in *3.Kp./SS-Aufkl.Abt.11* of the new SS division *'Nordland'*.

[2] Gösta Borg was born on August 14, 1915 in Stockholm, into a humble family. At fifteen he joined Furugård's National Socialist party. He later decided to pursue a military career, serving in the Swedish Royal Guard. During the Finnish-Soviet War, he volunteered for the Swedish Expeditionary Force and fought on the front lines. When Operation Barbarossa began in the summer of 1941, he crossed the Norwegian border to enlist in the *Waffen-SS*, together with his friend Ragnar Linner. The two were transferred to Sennheim and after a quick military education they were transferred to *Wiking*. After fighting from the fall of 1941 through the winter of 1942, both were wounded and discharged. After his recovery, however, Borg decided to enlist again. After returning to Germany, Borg was sent to the *SS-Junkerschule* in Bad Tölz, to follow the 3rd Officer Course for German Volunteers, which ended in March 1944. He was then assigned to the war correspondents unit of the *Waffen-SS*.

[3] E. Norling, *"Volontari svedesi nella Waffen-SS europea...."*, pagina 136

[4] E. Norling, *"Volontari svedesi nella Waffen-SS europea"*, pagina 143.

Bibliography

Massimiliano Afiero, *"I volontari stranieri di Hitler"*, Ritter editrice
Sven Erik Norling, *"Volontari svedesi nella Waffen-SS europea (1940-1945)"*, Novantico editrice

12.SS-Panzer-Division 'Hitlerjugend'
Formation of the division
by Massimiliano Afiero

Artur Axmann sitting amongst German youths.

Young members of the *Hitlerjugend*.

After the disastrous defeat of Stalingrad in February 1943, Adolf Hitler was persuaded to mobilize all available resources and forces to finally destroy Soviet Russia, calling on the German people to support *'Total-Krieg'*. The formation of the SS *Hitlerjugend* division was part of this great project of the *Führer*. The original idea was actually of the head of the Hitler Youth himself, Artur Axmann and of *SS-Gruppenführer* Gottlob Berger, head of the *SS-Hauptamt* (the Central Office of the SS) and responsible for enlistment in the *Waffen SS*. The plan was to create a new division of the *Waffen SS*, composed exclusively of volunteers from the *Hitlerjugend*, the organization that included all the German youth born in the year 1926. The new formation was to express the will of the same youth to sacrifice oneself for the achievement of the final victory.

On February 10, 1943, Adolf Hitler officially approved the formation of the new division. On February 13, the *Reichsführer-SS* Heinrich Himmler then sent a letter to *Reichsjugendführer* Artur Axmann to confirm the approval of the project: "... *I submitted to the* Führer *your offer about young people born in 1926, to form a division of volunteers for the* Waffen SS, *of the same value as the* Leibstandarte. *I also reported your desire to identify the division so as to clearly emphasize its origins and at the same time its affinity with the* Hitlerjugend. *The* Führer *was pleased and ordered me to make you start the recruitment of volunteers .... I proposed the name* 'Hitlerjugend' *for the division .... "*.

Himmler, center, and behind him to his right, *SS-Gruf.* Berger, during a visit to an SS unit.

Training of young members of the *Hitlerjugend.*

Training of young members of the *Hitlerjugend.*

After a series of meetings and discussions between Axmann, Berger and the other commanders of the *Waffen SS*, the following points were set for the formation of the division: Volunteers were to be recruited from young people born in the first half of 1926. The minimum height for the infantry units had to be at least 170 cm, for the signals units, armored crewmen, motorcyclists and in exceptional cases, if the boys had already received adequate training, of 168 cm. For the formation of the division, 840 officers and 4,000 non-commissioned officers were needed, of which a part had to come from the other formations of the *Waffen SS* and from army units. Axmann estimated that he could supply at least thirty thousand young people. They were to spend six weeks in *Waffen SS* training camps, then four weeks in the

Waffen-SS recruiting posters to urge youths to volunteer for the SS *Hitlerjugend* Division.

Reichsarbeitsdienst (Reich Labor Service = RAD), before joining the division. The recruitments that began in the spring, however, gave unsatisfactory results: many young people were less than 170 centimeters tall and some parents opposed the recruitment of their children. At the same time, the training weeks went from six to four and the RAD service was canceled.

The division was officially created on June 1, 1943. On the 24th, an order from the *SS-FHA* (*SS-Führungshauptamt*, the operational headquarters of the SS), established the final operational details for the division. The new unit was named *SS-Panzergrenadierdivision 'Hitlerjugend'*.

In that same month of June, one hundred and twenty officers of the *Leibstandarte* were assigned to the division, accompanied by several hundred non-commissioned officers. In addition, some units of the same *Leibstandarte* were transferred en bloc to the new division:

- *I.Abt./SS-Pz.Rgt. 'LSSAH'*
- *1.Kp./SS-Aufkl.-Abt. 'LSSAH'*
- *II.Abt./SS-Art.-Rgt. 'LSSAH'*

The formation of the new division developed under the supervision of the *SS-Ogruf.* Sepp Dietrich, commissioned in the spring of 1943, to also set up the future *I.SS-Panzer-Korps*, which was to include *LSSAH* and *Hitlerjugend*. One of Dietrich's goals was certainly to reorganize these two divisions together, making sure that each served as a reserve for the other, while preserving a body of officers and non-commissioned officers in common. The rest of the cadres were completed with reserve officers who had served in the Hitler Youth before the war.

SS-Brigdf. Fritz Witt.

SS-Hstuf. Heinrich Springer.

Division order of battle July 1943 (establishment phase)

Kommando, SS-Panzer-Grenadier-Division
SS-Pz.Gren.Rgt.1 'Hitlerjugend'
    I.-III.Bataillon
SS-Pz.Gren.Rgt.2 'Hitlerjugend'
    I.-III.Bataillon
SS-Panzer-Regiment 'Hitlerjugend'
SS-Artillerie-Rgt.(mot.) 'Hitlerjugend'
SS-Kradschützen-Regiment 'Hitlerjugend'
    I.-II.Bataillon
SS-Panzer-Jäger-Abteilung
SS-Flak-Abt.(mot.)
SS-Pionier-Btl.(mot.)
SS-Nachrichten-Abteilung (mot.)
SS-Pz.Gren.Ausbildungs und Ersatz-Btl.
SS-Div.Nachschub-Truppen
SS-Verwaltungs-Truppen
SS-Kraftfahrpark-Truppen
SS-Sanitäts-Truppen

Transfer to Beverloo

In July 1943, the division was sent to the Beverloo camp in Belgium. Recruitment was extended to volunteers born in the second half of 1926 to increase the number of staff, which was still insufficient. The recruits were dispensed from military training and work in the RAD and were directly transferred to the division. Before the war, no premilitary training was envisioned for the *Hitlerjugend*. *Reichsjugendführer* Baldur von Schirach had given greater emphasis to the artistic education of young people and to sports activities. Not until in 1942 was premilitary training introduced for young people between 16 and 18 years old. Military education was handled exclusively by the leaders of *Hitlerjugend*, all of whom were war veterans injured while serving at the front. A former head of the *Hitlerjugend* as well as an officer of the *Waffen SS*, *SS-Ustuf.* Herbert Taege, wrote on the subject: "... *the training program of the premilitary camps was restricted to 160 hours. It included small arms firing, maneuvering training, etc. At the end of this training the boys received the 'war training certificate', but it had nothing to do with the actual basic military education of the armed forces. "*

Very young members of the *Hitlerjugend* visiting members of the division while in training.

Training at the Beverloo camp, Summer 1943.

Considering that most of the young volunteers, veterans of four years of war, were in poor physical condition, the aide of the division (*Division Adjutant*), *SS-Stubaf.* Heinrich Springer, set the development of character and physical fitness as a priority in the training operations and only after that, the real military training. To solve the problem of the lack of 'specialist' officers, about fifty army officers were transferred to the division. For the military education of the *Hitlerjugend*, the Belgian camp of Beverloo, 72 kilometers southeast of Antwerp, was designated, as already mentioned, and initially, the recruits of the two *Panzergrenadier* regiments were trained here. Then only *SS-Pz.Gr.Rgt.25* was left while *SS-Pz.Gr.Rgt.26* was transferred to the training camp of Maria-Ter-Heide, fifteen kilometers northeast of Antwerp. The artillery regiment was quartered near the Beverloo camp, in the Mol area. The reconnaissance battalion and the medical detachment, commanded by *SS-Stubaf.* Rolf Schulz, were based in Turnhout, 48 kilometers northeast of Antwerp.

Training with anti-tank guns at the Beverloo camp. (US NARA)

Radio message training, 1943.

The pioneer battalion took up positions in Herentals on the Albert Canal, the logistics services in Geel, the panzer regiment at the Mailly-le-Camp training area, 35 kilometers south of Chalons-sur-Marne. Division HQ was located in Zwanestrand near Turnhout. *SS-Pz.Gren.A.-u.E.-Btl. 'HJ'*, the reinforcement and training battalion, was headquartered in Arnhem in the Netherlands.

The 12.SS-Panzerdivision 'Hitlerjugend'

Training was delayed for a while due to a lack of equipment. As of October 1, 1943, the division had only 7,540 rifles out of the 15,751 planned. The situation was even more critical for machine guns (431 out of 1,584), tanks (3 out of 198), armored infantry vehicles and armored cars (0 out of 347) and non-armored vehicles (12 out of 3,219). In October 1943, four *PzKpfw.IV* and two *PzKpfw.III* tanks were retrieved from the *Alkett* factories.

Training of new recruits under the direct supervision of Fritz Witt (right). (US NARA)

A motorcyclist of *Hitlerjugend* Division, 1943.

During the month of October it was decided to organize the division no longer as a formation of armored grenadiers, but as a panzer division (armored division) to be incorporated into the *I.SS-Panzer-Korps*. Existing personnel, weapons and equipment had to be used for the reorganization. So, on October 22, 1943, the division was renamed *12.SS-Panzerdivision 'Hitlerjugend'*. The two grenadier regiments were numbered 25 and 26, while all the other units were identified with the number 12. The unit was organized following the structure of a 1943 panzer division, structured with two regiments of armored grenadiers, one armored regiment, one regiment of artillery with four groups (one of which was equipped with self-propelled guns), a tank destroyer group, an anti-aircraft unit, a pioneer unit, a signals unit and the other service units. For this purpose, new units were created (in parentheses are the places where they were headquartered):

- *SS-Pz.Inst.-Abt.12* (at Turnhout)
- *SS-Begleit-Kp.12* (at Turnhout)
- *SS-Werfer-Abt. 12* (in Sterzing, then Enghien)
- *SS-Pz.Rgt.12* (in France, in Mailly-le-Camp then transferred to Holland, in Hasselt, in January 1944)
- *SS-StuG-Abt.12* (dissolved in March 1944)

Division order of battle (Nov. 1943)

Kommando, SS-Panzer-Division
 Stab der Division
 SS-Div. Kartenstelle (mot.)
   SS-Feldendarmerie-Kp. (mot.) 12

A *Hitlerjugend* soldier during training, 1943 (*C. Trang*).

SS-Panzer-Grenadier-Regiment 25
I.-III.SS.Inf.Btl (mot.)
13.Inf.Geschütz-Kompanie
14.le.Flak.Kp.(Sf)
15.Pionier-Kompanie
SS-Panzer-Grenadier-Regiment 26
I.-II.SS.Inf.Btl (mot.)
III.SS-Inf.Btl. (gep.)
13.Inf.Geschütz-Kompanie
14.le.Flak.Kp.(Sf)
15.Pionier-Kompanie
SS-Panzer-Regiment 12
I.SS-Pz.Abt.
    Stabs-Kompanie
    1.-4.Pz.Kp.
    Panzer-Werkstatt-Zug
    II.SS-Pz.Abt.
    Stabs-Kompanie
    Panzer-Flamm-Zug

        5.-8.Pz.Kp.
Panzer-Werkstatt-Kompanie
SS-Panzer-Aufklärungs-Abteilung 12
Stabs-Kompanie
1.-2.Panzer-Späh-Kompanie
3.-4.Pz.Aufkl.Kompanie
5.s.Pz.Aufkl.Kompanie
Versorgungs-Kompanie
SS-Panzer-Jäger-Abteilung 12
Stabs-Kompanie (Sf)
1.-3.Pz.Jg.Kompanie (Sf)
SS-Werfer-Abt.(mot.) 12
Stabs-Batterie
1.-4.Nebelwerfer-Batterie (mot.)
le.Nebelwerfer-Kolonne (mot.)
SS-Panzer-Pionier-Btl.12
Stab
1.Pz.Pi.Kompanie
2.-3.Pz.Pi.Kompanie (mot.)
Pz.-Br.Kol. (Brückengerät 'K')
Pz.-Br.Kol. (Brückengerät 'B')
SS-Panzer-Nachrichten-Abteilung 12
Stab
Pz.Fernsprech-Kompanie
Pz.Funk-Kompanie
Leichte Nachrichten-Kolonne
SS-Panzer-Artillerie-Regiment 12
Stabs-Batterie (mot.)
I.SS-Artillerie-Abteilung (Sf)

Training for Artillery observers, 1943.

SS-Ostuf. **Gerd Bremer.**

Stabs-Batterie (mot.)
1.-2.Btt. (Sf) (6 Sd Kfz 124 'Wespe')
3.Btt. (Sf) (6 Sd Kfz 165 'Hummel')
II.SS-Artillerie-Abteilung (mot.)
Stabs-Batterie
4.-5.Batterie (105mm)
III.SS-Artillerie-Abteilung (mot.)
Stabs-Batterie
6.-7.Batterie (105mm)
IV.SS-Artillerie-Abteilung (mot.)
Stabs-Batterie
8.-9.Batterie (150mm)
10.Batterie (105mm)
SS-Flak-Abteilung (mot.) 12
Stab
1.Flak-Batterie (mot.) (9 37mm)
2.-4.Flak-Batterie (mot.) (4 88mm and 3 20mm)
Flak-Scheinwerfer-Staffel (4 60cm)
SS-Feldersatz-Bataillon 12
Stab
1.-5.Kompanie
SS-Division-Nachschub-Truppen (mot.)
Stab
1.-7.Kraftwagen-Kompanie
leichte Flak-Batterie
Werstatt-Kompanie
Versorgungs-Kompanie
SS-Kraftfahrpark-Truppen
Stab
1.-3.Werstatt-Kompanie (mot.)
Ersatzteil-Kolonne
SS-Verwaltungs-Truppen
Stab
Schlächterei-Kompanie
Bäckerei-Kompanie
Verpflegungs-Amt
Feldpostamt
SS-Sanitäts-Truppen
Stab
1.-2-Sanitäts-Kompanie (mot.)
1.-3.Krankenkraftwagen-Zug

Training of the units continues

With the move to the Beverloo training camp, the young *Hitlerjugend* volunteers entered an occupied country for the first time. Those who were quartered at the Leopoldsburg camp initially had minimal contact with the local population. Among the volunteers, there were also some Flemings enrolled in the *Waffen SS*, the only ones who really felt at home. Most of the men were quartered in towns and villages in barracks, schools or hotels. The Allied air force supplied the partisan formations in occupied Belgium with weapons and equipment and the *Hitlerjugend* units were occasionally engaged in sweep operations.

Training with *Wespe* self-propelled howitzer at the Beverloo camp, Summer 1943.

Training with *Flak* gun for these young soldiers, 1943.

Meanwhile, all the training of the new recruits was aimed at rapid engagement in battle, while basic training was reduced to a bare minimum. After completing the individual training for the volunteers of the first contingent, the division issued *Ausbildungsbefehl Nr. 1* (training order number 1) on November 17, 1943: in it, the guidelines for the continuation of collective training were given, in squads, platoons and companies. This next phase was completed at the beginning of December 1943. Between 5 and 7 December 1943, at the invitation of the divisional commander, *Reichsjugendführer* Artur Axmann visited *Hitlerjugend* and was very impressed with the level of training achieved by his 'lads'. Training in the use of weapons, rifles, pistols and machine guns, took up a significant part of the instruction. Volunteers were trained in the open field simulating real battle conditions.

General der Panzertruppen, Leo Frhr. Geyr von Schweppenburg, responsible for training the division, was very impressed by these maneuvers in the field. The General paid close attention to camouflage, radio codes and close combat at night.

November 1943: Swearing-in ceremony of new recruits for *SS-Pz.Gr.Rgt. 25*, in the presence of Kurt Meyer, in the background. (US NARA)

A *Hitlerjugend Panther* during training, 1943.

In January 1944, the situation improved with the arrival of vehicles taken from the Italian army. But the lack of fuel remained critical and significantly impaired staff training. On the other hand, individual training could be considered excellent. In February 1944, when the first divisional exercises began, the HJ fielded more than twenty thousand men, whose average age,

in World War Two 1939-1945

SS-Sturmbannführer Max Wünsche on his *Panther*.

The *PzKpfw.IV '635'* of *SS-Oscha*. Terdenge (BA).

A *Hitlerjugend PzKpfw.IV* crew during training, 1944.

including officers and NCOs, was 18! Their morale was extraordinarily high and this was confirmed during their later employment in Normandy. Equipment finally began to arrive and in large quantities and so at that time, *SS-Pz.Rgt.12* had 97 *PzKpfw.IV* and only 8 *PzKpfw.V 'Panther'*.

Formation of the Panzer-Regiment

The personnel for the Panzer Abteilung came from the *I.Pz.Abteilung* of the *Leibstandarte*, detached from the division at the beginning of April 1943. In fact, immediately after the end of the fighting for Kharkov, between the end of March and the beginning of April, *I./SS-Pz.Rgt. 1* was sent, to Berlin to be re-equipped with the new *PzKpfw.V Panther*. Headquartered at the Berlin-Lichterfelde barracks, the battalion received a new transfer order in early May, with all its staff, 412 officers, non-commissioned officers and soldiers, to Mailly-le-Camp, France. In mid-June, Dietrich placed *SS-Sturmbannführer* Max Wünsche, hitherto commander of the *I./SS-Pz.Rgt.1*, in command of the new *SS-Panzer-Regiment 'Wünsche'*. The cadres and 50% of the initial staff came from *I./SS-Pz.Rgt.1*. A core of 15 officers, 44 non-commissioned officers and 146 men was assigned to the new armored regiment planned for the new division. At the end of June, a large contingent of recruits, trained in Bitche by the *SS-Panzer-Ausbildungs-und Ersatz-Regiment* detached battalion in the Moselle, arrived at Mailly-le-Camp. This training area was a few hundred kilometers from the Beverloo camp, where the first contingents destined for the ranks of the *Hitlerjugend-Division* in Belgium were transferred between July and August. Meanwhile, *SS-Stubaf.* Wünsche was transferred to the Wünsdorf Armored Troop School near Berlin to take a course for armored regiment commanders from 28 July to 20 August 1943.

The crews of the 5.*Kompanie* of II.SS-Pz.Rgt.12 lined up in front of their 'new' *PzKpfw IV Ausf H* for inspection. The vehicles are painted in dark yellow with a green and brown camouflage pattern. All crew members wear leather jackets and trousers from the Royal Italian Navy. (*Michael Cremin collection*)

SS-Ostuf. **Rudolf von Ribbentrop.**

The actual formation of *SS-Panzer Regiment 12* therefore did not begin until the end of July, when beginning with the first nucleus of personnel available, a final force of 71 officers, 850 non-commissioned officers and 1,380 men was reached. *SS-Stubaf.* Wünsche busied himself preparing his armored units. Other officers from the *Leibstandarte*, such as *SS-Hstuf.* Karl Heinz Prinz, in command of *II.Pz.Abt.* and *SS-Hstuf.* Arnold Jürgensen in command of *I.Pz.Abt.* assisted him in this task. Among the names of the company commanders that stood out were Rudolf von Ribbentrop, the son of the German Foreign Minister, recipient of the Knight's Cross received on 15 July 1943 as *SS-Ostuf.* and commander of the *6./SS-Pz.Rgt. 1 "LSSAH"* and

Hans Siegel. Wünsche hoped that the new division would be equipped with the latest panzer models, but instead of the *Tiger* tanks, only 'old' *Panthers* and even older *PzKpfw IVs* arrived at the regiment. The crews of the tanks also received *Kriegsmarine* uniforms intended for the crews of the *U-Boote*, material originally of the Italian Navy seized by the Germans after 8 September 1943.

A *Hitlerjugend Panther* from MAN factory of Nuremberg (*Hubert Meyer Collection*).

Wünsche did not lose heart and continued to train his men with great spirit and energy, trying to make up for the lack of more modern and powerful equipment with a high level of training. To better educate his men in the knowledge of their vehicles, he sent them to the MAN tank factory in Nuremberg for periods of 8-14 days: there, the aspiring tankers worked 12 hours a day actively participating in the construction of the tanks, viewing the whole manufacturing process to fully learn all the 'secrets' of the vehicles, but above all their actual potential and their limits. Other men were sent to practice firing at the Putlos range, for *Flak* practice in Schongau, for driving at the *Waffen SS* Motor Vehicle Institute in Vienna, for transmissions to the Friedrichshafen gearbox factory. Special attention was paid to the training of mechanics and vehicle maintenance personnel. The situation progressively improved with the arrival of another seven *Panzer IVs*. Regimental companies were then formed and a first issue of equipment was carried out. As of December 1, 1943, the *SS-Panzer-Regiment* had ten operational *Panzer IVs* and one *Panzer IV* under repair. During the same month, the arrival of another 29 new Panzer IVs allowed *SS-Ogruf.* Dietrich to distribute these vehicles to the various companies during his inspection tour. On December 10, *Reichsjugendführer* Artur Axmann came to inspect the regiment. As of January 1, 1944, 38 *Panzer IVs* were operational and two more were under repair. Also in early January 1944, the *Panzer-Regiment* was transferred from Mailly-le-Camp to the division's assembly area in Belgium. The personnel were placed in the Hasselt area, 57 kilometers southeast of Antwerp, near the Beverloo camp.

PzKpfw IVs of 6./SS-Pz.Rgt.12 during a halt in a Flemish village during an exercise. (US NARA)

A *Sturmgeschütz-Ausbildungs-Batterie*, seconded to the *SS-Panzer-Division Hohenstaufen* for instruction, was subordinated to *II./SS-Pz.Rgt.12*. By the time the last convoy departed from Mailly-le-Camp, a *Panther* and 20 *Panzer IVs* had been assigned the regiment between January 7-8, followed by 15 *Panzer IVs* on January 13 for *II./SS-Pz. Rgt 12*, then another 15 again on January 20. A first exercise by II.Abteilung was carried out from 25 January near Hasselt. At that time, *I./SS-Pz.Rgt.12* left its billeting area in Beverloo to move to Hasselt. On January 30, *SS-Stubaf.* Wünsche was officially promoted to the rank of *SS-Obersturmbannführer*. Training continued with difficulty due to a lack of practice ammunition and fuel. On February 3 and 5, *SS-Panzer-Regiment 12* reported a total of 79 *Panzer IVs* and 7

Panthers in operation, while another 18 *Panzer IVs* and 1 *Panther* were under repair. On February 6, part of the regiment conducted a field exercise in the presence of *Generaloberst* Guderian, General von Geyr and *SS-Ogruf.* Dietrich. The future delivery of more panzers depended heavily on the outcome of the exercise itself.

Von Rundstedt (from behind) and Sepp Dietrich visiting division personnel. Gerd Bremer is on the left and Mohnke on the right. A flamethrower half-track is in the background. (US NARA)

Another moment during Dietrich and von Rundstedt's visit, with Kurt Meyer and Fritz Witt. (US NARA)

At the same time, an exercise of *I./SS-Pz.Gr.Rgt.25* was conducted, with live ammunition, with the participation of a battery of the artillery regiment, again in the presence of the three senior officers. Despite the excellent performance of the men, the division continued to suffer a severe shortage of weapons, materials, vehicles and fuel. Between the end of March and the beginning of April, *Hitlerjugend* received the order to move to Normandy, following the departure of the *Frundsberg* and the *Hohenstaufen* for the Galician front. The armored regiment was to embark from four stations, consisting of 17 convoys, beginning on 31 March. It was headquartered in the region of Louviers, with Wünsche's command post in Acquigny. On 12 April, the *Panzerflak-Zug*, equipped with 12 *Flakpanzer 38 (t)* armed with *2cm Flak 38* pieces, arrived from its training in Germany at an army unit based in Schwetzingen, *3. (Pz.Fla) Kompanie* of *Panzer-Ersatz-und Ausbildungs-Abteilung 204*, was integrated into the regiment. As of April 20, *I./SS-Panzer-Regiment 12* led by *SS-Stubaf.* Jürgensen, had 26 *Panthers* on issue, of which 23 operational.

A *Hitlerjugend Flakpanzer 38 (t)* on Western Front, 1944.

SS-Stubaf. Jürgensen.

SS-Ogruf. Sepp Dietrich and *SS-Brigdf.* Fritz Witt.

On the same day, *SS-Ostubaf.* Wünsche, who was part of the *I./SS-Pz.Korps* delegation sent on an official visit to Hitler's headquarters on the occasion of his birthday, handed over to the *Führer* a gift from Sepp Dietrich's armored corps of 2,006 million *Reichsmarks* and he took the opportunity to show him photos of an anti-aircraft defense tank armed with a 2cm *Flakvierling*. This new vehicle was devised by the *Hitlerjugend* regiment, which had brilliantly mounted a *Flakvierling* on the chassis of a *Panzer IV*. This prototype served as the basis for the development of the future *Flakpanzer IV Wirbelwind*. Two other *Flakpanzer IVs* thus completed the equipment issue of these *Panzerflak-Zug* to be assigned to *II./SS-Pz.Rgt.*

Hitlerjugend PzKpfw.IV, **Spring 1944 (*Bundesarchiv*).**

Between 27 and 29 April, major maneuvers took place at the divisional level in Louviers, with *I./SS-Panzer-Regiment 12* and in the presence of *Generaloberst* Heinz Guderian, *General der Panzertruppe* Leo Geyr von Schweppenburg, commander of *Panzergruppe West* and *SS-Obergruppenführer* Dietrich. At the end of April, the division was considered operational and ready for the front, although its tank equipment was not yet complete. As of April 30, *SS-Panzer-Regiment 12* mustered 6 *Panzer II*, 1 *Panzer IV L/24* (short gun), 3 *Panzer IV L/43* (long gun), 90 *Panzer IV L/48*, 26 *Panther* and 3 *Flakpanzer IV* with 2cm *Flakvierling*.

In May, *12.SS-Panzer-Division Hitlerjugend* had to cede 2,042 men, including 13 officers, to *1.SS-Panzer-Division 'LSSAH'* undergoing reorganization in Belgium. *SS-Panzer-Regiment 12* ceded six officers and 400 soldiers and NCOs to its sister division. On May 21, eight *Panthers* arrived for the *I. Abteilung*, followed by another convoy with another eight, two days later. On May 31, two new convoys each transported seven Panzer Vs to Louviers station. On June 1, 1944, the *Hitlerjugend* was considered operational. On the same day, the *Panzer-Regiment* fielded up 91 *Panzer IVs* and 48 operational *Panthers*, as well as 7 *Panzer IVs* and 2 *Panthers* under repair. The holdings of *Panthers* had significantly improved with the supply of 30 tanks at the end of May, a few days before the landing. The training of the *Hitlerjugend* continued and the signs of an impending Allied invasion multiplied. And so it was that on June 3, *SS-Ostuf.* von Ribbentrop was wounded aboard his *Kübelwagen*, strafed by Allied planes flying at low altitude.

The divisional coat of arms

The divisional coat of arms was expressly chosen thinking of the incorporation of the unit as part of *I.SS-Panzer-Korps*, which also included the *Leibstandarte Adolf Hitler*. The emblem was the result of a mini-competition that began on November 10, 1943, and was won by *SS-Rottenführer* Franz Lang of *Abteilung V* (transport) of the divisional staff. All vehicles in the division, from motorbikes to *Panther* tanks, received the emblem painted in white. The members of the division enthusiastically welcomed the choice of the emblem, which made them feel very close to their comrades in the *Leibstandarte*. A cuff band with the inscription *'Hitlerjugend'* had already been approved for the division in June 1943, but it was delivered to the units only after the fighting in Normandy, so personnel from the *Leibstandarte* or other SS formations continued to carry the cuff band of their unit of origin.

Bibliography

Massimiliano Afiero, "*12.SS-Panzer-Division Hitlerjugend*", Associazione Culturale Ritterkreuz
Massimiliano Afiero, "*12th SS Panzer Division Hitlerjugend: From Formation to the Battle of Caen*", Casemate Pub & Book Dist Llc